BUT HE GIVETH MORE GRACE

BY TOM HARMON

BUT HE GIVETH MORE GRACE
ISBN 9781609200749
Printed in the United States of America
©2013 Tom Harmon
All rights reserved

Cover design by Isaac Publishing, Inc.
Interior design by Sunny B. DiMartino and Isaac Publishing, Inc.

Library of Congress Cataloging-in-Publication Data

API
Ajoyin Publishing, Inc.
P.O. 342
Three Rivers, MI 49093
www.ajoyin.com

Please direct your inquiries to admin@ajoyin.com

CONTENTS

Foreword 1

Preface. 3

CHAPTER ONE   Who's the "He" 5

CHAPTER TWO   What Grace Is This? 25

CHAPTER THREE Grace for Salvation 41

CHAPTER FOUR   Grace for Sanctification 51

CHAPTER FIVE   Grace for Speaking 65

CHAPTER SIX   Grace for Suffering 75

CHAPTER SEVEN Grace for Singing 89

FOREWORD

The very word "grace" has become a sweet sounding word to me. I love how it is used in Scripture to describe the things that I have come to cherish: "The God of all grace", "The word of His grace", "The grace of God that bringeth salvation", "The Spirit of grace", "The grace of Christ", "Justified freely by His grace" and "Salvation by grace". It's no wonder the hymn writers used adjectives like "Amazing grace" "Wonderful grace" and "Marvelous grace" just to name a few. I believe a person's entire theology is shaped by their understanding of the grace of God. It has been my privilege from early in my journey of faith to sit under preachers and Bible teachers who taught the scriptural foundations of the doctrines of grace. This attempt at writing on the vast subject of grace will be good for me. I am sure the discipline of study, preaching, and writing on this topic will help me grow in grace. The Apostle Peter closed his second and final letter with the exhortation, "But grow in the grace, and in the knowledge of our Lord and Savior, Jesus Christ. To him be glory both now and forever. Amen" (2 Pet. 3:18). It is an encouragement to know we can grow in grace. The Apostle Paul in his last letter to Timothy encouraged him on the subject of grace, "Thou, therefore, my son, be strong in the grace that is in Christ Jesus" (2 Tim. 2:1). To grow in grace, to become strong in grace, is all done by His grace! May His grace and peace be multiplied to us as we consider "BUT HE GIVETH MORE GRACE."

ACKNOWLEDGMENTS

I would like to recognize the following people for their help with completing this book:

Edited by Bob English
Cover photo taken by Joyce Harmon
Back photo by David DeJong
Proofread by Mary Evenson
Cover layout by Ajoyin Publishing

But he giveth more grace. Wherefore he saith, God resisteth the proud, but gieth grace unto the humble. –James 4:6

PREFACE

It is important to know that God declares Himself to be gracious by nature. For example when Moses was on Mount Sinai with God and the people of Israel had committed the horrible sin of making and worshiping the golden calf , God threatened to destroy them but then relented (see Ex. 32:1–14). Later, He revealed He changed His decision because He is "The Lord, the Lord God, merciful and gracious, longsuffering, and abundant in goodness and truth" (Ex. 34:6). An appeal for more grace is largely based on knowing the gracious nature of God.

Another truth we must acknowledge when considering the grace of God is God's sovereign control over His administration of grace. After the events mentioned above, Moses earnestly begged God to show him His glory, to which God responded, "I will make all my goodness pass before you, and I will proclaim the name of the Lord before you, and will be gracious to whom I will be gracious, and show mercy on whom I will show mercy" (Ex. 33:19). God thereby set forth that He alone determines and controls the administration of His grace.

King David, with his feet of clay, understood the gracious nature of God as well as His sovereign administration of grace. After David had illegitimately fathered a child with Bathsheba, the child was struggling for life. David fasted and prayed for the child to live. But when the child died David said, "While the child was yet alive, I fasted and wept; for I said, 'Who can tell whether God will be gracious to me, that the child may live? But now he is dead, why should I fast? Can I bring him back again? I shall go to him, but he shall not return to me" (2 Sam. 12:22–23). David's statement demonstrates that he could trust in God's authority to withhold His grace when it suits His sovereign purpose. We are growing in grace when we understand He is God and we are not, that His ways are higher than our ways and His thoughts than our thoughts.

CHAPTER ONE

WHO'S THE "HE"

The title of this book comes from the first part of James 4:6, "BUT HE GIVETH MORE GRACE". In this first chapter we must establish who the "He" is who gives grace. James continues, "Wherefore he saith, God resisteth the proud, but giveth grace unto the humble … . Submit yourselves, therefore, to God. … Draw near to God, and he will draw near to you. …" (vv. 6–8). The context therefore indicates the "He" is God. In a pluralistic world of so many gods, one might ask which god? If we miss the answer to this question, grace has no meaning for us. The God of the Bible is the God of ALL grace. "But the God of all grace, who hath called us unto his eternal glory by Christ Jesus, after ye have suffered awhile, make you perfect, establish, strengthen, settle you. To him be glory and dominion forever and ever. Amen" (1 Pet. 5:10–11).

The "He" we will focus on in this book is the God of the Bible. The Bible is God's resume. Man in his search for meaning begins with the premise that he himself is kind of a small god. A small god conducting job interviews for someone worthy of being the big god. When the God of all grace is asked what His job qualifications are He hands us His resume. His resume begins with "In the beginning God ..." Let's stop there for a moment and try to imagine the scope of that statement. In the first four words of Genesis God is declaring His existence, He is not debating it. God isn't saying He began in the beginning but rather He was in the beginning before the beginning began. You can't think on that statement very long before it leaves your capacity to comprehend. In my mental framework everything has a beginning and an end, yet in the first four words of His resume the God of all grace just stepped outside of my ability to comprehend. This is His claim, He never tries to prove it; you can take it or leave it. From His very first words, it is all a matter of faith.

The Eternal One

He was in the beginning before the beginning began. "In the beginning was the Word, and the Word was with God, and the Word was God. The same was in the beginning with God" (John 1:1–2, emphasis mine). Before the very foundations of the world, the God of the Bible was. When God told the apostle John to write some history in advance, He once again asserted His claim of being the eternal one. "I am Alpha and Omega, the beginning and the ending, saith the Lord, who is, and who was, and who is to come, the Almighty" (Rev. 1:8). The apostle Paul wrote to the church in Colossae about the beginning of time. Once again without hesitation, we see God being before the beginning. "And he is before all things, and by him all things consist" (Col. 1:17).

When the apostle Paul charged young Timothy with the responsibility of setting things in order in the churches of Asia, he emphasized the need for teaching sound doctrine. "As I besought thee to abide still at Ephesus, when I went into

Macedonia, that thou mighest charge some that they teach no other doctrine" (1 Tim. 1:3). "For fornicators, for them that defile themselves with mankind, for kidnappers, for liars, for perjured persons, and if there be any other thing that is contrary to sound doctrine" (1 Tim. 1:10). " If thou put the brethren in remembrance of these things, thou shalt be a good minister of Jesus Christ, nourished up in the words of faith and of good doctrine, unto which thou hast attained" (1 Tim. 4:6). "Till I come, give attendance to reading, to exhortation, to doctrine" (1 Tim. 4:13). "Take heed unto thyself and unto the doctrine; continue in them; for in doing this thou shalt both save thyself and them that hear thee" (1 Tim. 4:16). The eternality of God is a major part of the sound doctrine Paul wanted Timothy to emphasize. "Now unto the King eternal, immortal, invisible, the only wise God, be honor and glory forever. Amen" (1 Tim. 1:17). God wastes no time. I mean right out of the gate in Genesis, He claims to be the eternal one. Eternity puts Him in a class all by Himself, high and lifted up beyond all His competitors and, I must add, beyond all human comprehension, demanding faith in nothing more than His Word. But "He" giveth more grace.

THE CREATOR

Apparently without hesitation or apology God claims position as Creator. He does not tip toe into His qualifications. "In the beginning God created the heaven and the earth" (Gen. 1:1). That one verse more than exhausts my capacity to comprehend. Imagine if I could understand the broad expanse of heaven and the finest secrets of earth. I can't even come close, yet God claims to have created it all. The first two chapters of Genesis give the details of how He created all things but before we consider some of that let's look at why He created it. "For by him were all things created, that are in heaven, and that are in earth, visible and invisible, whether they be thrones, or dominions, or principalities, or powers—all things were created by him, and for him" (Col. 1:16). God had Himself in mind when He created all things. He didn't create things for the things' sake: He created them for Himself and His pleasure, including man.

How Did God Create

On the first day God created light. "And God said, Let there be light: and there was light. And God saw the light, that it was good: and God divided the light from the darkness. And God called the light Day, and the darkness he called Night. And the evening and the morning were the first day" (Gen. 1:3–6). God created all things by the power of His word. He basically used the same method throughout those first six days of creation. It appears He didn't need more than six days to complete the job and on the seventh day He rested, "For in six days the Lord made heaven and earth, the sea, and all that in them is, and rested the seventh day; wherefore, the Lord blessed the Sabbath day, and hallowed it" (Ex. 20:11).

I believe the Bible teaches a literal six day creation. I arrived at this largely from relying on a basic rule of interpretation which is the plain literal sense of a passage should be accepted unless the form or context indicates otherwise. I've heard it said, "Keep the plain things the main things and the main things the plain things." I have dear friends in the ministry who have room for an old earth theory. I have others who consider themselves "evolutionary creationists". Although I don't agree with them on their position, I exercise the grace given to me in Scripture, "With all lowliness and meekness, with long-suffering, for-bearing one another in love, Endeavoring to keep the unity of the Spirit in the bond of peace" (Eph. 4:2–3). On this side of heaven I doubt all Christians will ever have unity of theology; but by the grace of God, born again people are called to maintain the unity of the Spirit. Each person must live off his own theology and what they believe the Bible accurately teaches on any multitude of subjects.

I believe the evening and morning spoken of in Genesis was the same 24 hour time frame we speak of today. What about the earth seeming to be so old? I believe when God created things He gave them age. When He made man, He didn't make a boy, but a fully mature man. He did the same with the woman and everything else: birds, insects, reptiles, cattle, horses, etc. God made a fully mature oak tree with acorns on it. There is no indication He made an acorn and waited for it to mature into an oak. He made a chicken full of eggs rather than an egg which needed to be incubated. He made the birds, each with their unique feathers, colors, sizes, songs, migratory patterns and nesting habits. The eggs that were in them would produce other birds after their kind. He made all the different kinds of fish with the same ability to reproduce after their kind. He made all the plants with seeds in them after their kind, ready for reproduction. I believe God made things with age and chose to preserve them through an ability to reproduce after their kind. "Thou, even thou, art Lord alone; thou hast made heaven, the heaven of heavens, with all their host, the earth, and all things that are in it, the seas, and all that is in them, and thou preservest them all; and the host of heaven worshipeth thee" (Neh.9:6).

In humility I can say I don't understand all the mysteries of the universe, but I do want to take what seems obvious and go with it. Doing so makes room for allowing God to be bigger than my ability to comprehend. One should always see God as bigger than his theology. The literal six day approach to creation kind of sets the stage for me in how the word "day" is normally used in scripture. For example, the Bible speaks of a resurrection day. Jesus was with His disciples when He received the news that His friend Lazarus had died. Two days later He told His disciples they were going back to Bethany to wake up His friend Lazarus because he was sleeping. The disciples were reluctant to go and used the excuse that if he was sleeping he must be doing better. Jesus told them plainly that Lazarus was dead and He was glad for their sakes that he was. He wanted to strengthen their faith by showing His power over death. Lazarus' sister Martha met Jesus first. She wished He could have arrived earlier, for if He had He could have saved him. When Jesus made it clear that he was going to rise again, she responds with good theology. "Martha saith unto him, I know that he shall rise again in the resurrection at the last day" (John 11:24). I believe the day she made reference to is a future event that will occur during an appointed 24 hour day. "Behold, I show you a mystery: We shall not all sleep, but we shall all be changed, In a moment, in the twinkling of an eye, at the last trump; for the trumpet shall sound, and the dead shall be raised incorruptible, and we shall be changed" (1 Cor. 15:51–52).

Jesus had a birth*day*. "For unto you is born this *day* in the city of David a Savior, who is Christ the Lord" (Luke 2:11). Jesus had a death *day* and a resurrection *day*. "Thus it is written, and thus it behooved Christ to suffer, and to rise from the dead the third *day*" (Lu. 24:46). There was a *day* Jesus ascended up into heaven. "The former treatise have I made, O Theophilus, of all that Jesus began both to do and teach, until the *day* in which he was taken up, after he, through the Holy Spirit, had given commandments unto the apostles whom he had chosen; To whom also he showed himself alive after his passion by many infallible proofs, being seen by them forty *days*, and speaking of the things pertaining to the kingdom of God" (Acts 1:1–3). The Holy Spirit came on the *day* of Pentecost and the church was birthed. "And when the *day* of Pentecost was fully come, they were all with one accord in one place" (Acts 2:1). It may be too simple of an approach, but so far it has been helpful for me not to look too far beyond the obvious.

The Heavens

On the fourth day, God made the sun, moon, and stars. "And God said, Let there be lights in the firmament of the heaven to divide the day from the night; and let them be for signs, and for seasons, and for days, and years; and let them be for lights in the firmament of the heaven to give light upon the earth; and it was so. And God made two great lights; the greater light to rule the day, and the lesser light to rule the night: he made the stars also. And God set them in the firmament of the heaven to give light upon the earth" (Gen. 1:14–17). The sun, moon, and stars shout of design. If we were one degree closer to the sun, the earth would become a desert, a desolate and barren wasteland. If we were one degree farther from the sun, the planet would become a block of ice. The earth rotates at 66,000 mph. The moon's gravitational pull stabilizes the earth, keeping it spinning in precise balance. If the moon were removed from our solar system the earth would soon begin to wobble violently and eventually come apart. When man ponders the heavens, he hears God's voice. "When I consider thy heavens, the works of thy fingers, the moon and the stars, which thou hast ordained, What is man, that thou art mindful of him? And the son of man, that thou visitest him?" (Psa. 8:3–4). There are over 100 billion stars in our moderately-sized galaxy and there are over 100 billion galaxies in the universe. You can hold a dime at arm's length, point it toward heaven in any direction, and hide 15 million stars behind it. If you could travel at the speed of light (186,000 miles per/second), you could circle the earth seven times in one second. You could travel to the moon in a little over a second. But it would still take you over four years to travel to the nearest star. In His resume, it is recorded in a "by the way" manner, "He made the stars also". But "<u>He</u>" giveth more grace.

The Earth

The sun, moon, and stars were made to give light upon the earth, thus it would appear that planet earth is the darling of the Creator's eye. There is such detail in the earth and such a complex relationship among earth's created things from plants, soil, air, water, temperature, to living creatures and man. Design is stamped over all of it. The world cannot be just a series of accidents left to time and chance as the evolutionist would like us to believe. To what end would life be? What reason other than to be born, exist for a short breath called life, and end up as worm food? Would it all be only to continue the propagation of the species for another 3½ billion years? Creation speaks of design. That design gives man meaning and purpose. If my origin is found in a God who made me, then my destiny is also found in Him. If we never looked up but only looked around us at the things of earth, it would be sufficient to acknowledge a Maker.

The apostle Paul used this reasoning when he spoke to the men of Athens on Mar's Hill overlooking the Pantheon which was filled with fetishes of all kinds of man-made gods. "For as I passed by, and beheld your devotions, I found an altar with this inscription, TO THE UNKNOWN GOD. Whom, therefore, ye ignorantly worship, him declare I unto you. God, who made the world and all things in it, seeing that he is Lord of heaven and earth, dwelleth not in temples made with hands, neither is worshiped with men's hands, as though he needed anything, seeing he giveth to all life, and breath, and all things" (Acts 17:23–25). The earth has given the Creator a platform that is hard to ignore. "Because that which may be known of God is manifest in them; for God hath shown it unto them. For the invisible things of him from the creation of the world are clearly seen, being understood by the things that are made, even his eternal power and Godhead, so that they are without excuse" (Rom. 1:19–20).

MAN

"And God said, Let us make man in our own image, after our likeness; and let them have dominion over the fish of the sea, and over the fowl of the air, and over the cattle, and over all the earth, and over every creeping thing that creepeth upon the earth. So God created man in his own image, in the image of God created he him; male and female created he them" (Gen. 1:26–27). If planet earth is the darling of the Creator's eye, what value must He place on man to have given him rule over all the earth? "And the Lord God formed man of the dust of the ground, and breathed into his nostrils the breath of life; and man became a living soul" (Gen. 2:7). God made man in His likeness, but not in His exactness. God gave man a spirit that enabled him to have fellowship with his Maker. "God is a Spirit; and they that worship him must worship him in spirit and in truth" (John 4:24). All the religions of the world show evidence to the spirit of a man and his need to worship in spirit. God created man to worship in spirit and truth but instead man was fooled when he believed the lie of Satan—the lie that he could be like God. "Because, when they knew God, they glorified him not as God, neither were thankful, but became vain in their imaginations, and their foolish heart was darkened. Professing themselves to be wise, they became fools, and changed the glory of the incorruptible God into an image made like corruptible man, and birds, and four-footed beasts, and creeping things" (Rom. 1:21–23).

The Egyptians of Moses' day worshiped the Nile River and said it was sacred. The Nile is not sacred; the One who made the Nile is sacred. They also worshiped the sun; the sun is not sacred, the One who made the sun is sacred. They worshiped cattle and made figures of half man and half cow. Neither man nor cattle are sacred; the One who made them is sacred. Different people groups throughout the world have worshiped mountains or volcanoes calling them sacred. Others have worshiped trees or animals, such as lions, tigers, buffalo, crocodiles, etc. None of these things are sacred, only the One Who made these things is sacred and worthy of worship. "Thou art worthy, O Lord, to receive glory and honor and power; for thou hast created all things, and for thy pleasure they are and were created" (Rev. 4:11). Worshipping in spirit must be accompanied by truth; otherwise, we are as deceived as Adam was in the garden. "Who exchanged the truth of God for a lie, and worshiped and served the creature more than the Creator, who is blessed forever. Amen" (Rom. 1:25).

WHY THE COMMANDMENT

After the Creator made man He placed him in the Garden and gave him a single commandment. Some may ask, "Why did God give the Commandment?" I ask, "Why not give the Commandment? Hath not the potter power over the clay?" Though God gave man dominion over all the earth he made no bones about His dominion over man. "And the Lord God took the man, and put him into the Garden of Eden to till it and to keep it. And the Lord God commanded the man, saying, Of every tree of the garden thou mayest freely eat; But of the tree of the knowledge of good and evil, thou shalt not eat of it; for in the day that thou eatest thereof thou shalt surely die" (Gen. 2:15–17). If God did not create man, He has no right to rule him. If God has no right to rule him, He has no right to judge him. If He has no right to judge him, the Cross is absolutely meaningless. The crescendo of God's resume is the Cross of Jesus Christ. It is no wonder Satan attacks the doctrine of creation with such a vengeance. We will unpack this with greater detail in a moment.

OTHER GODS

The first commandment Moses received on Mt. Sinai concerned other gods. "Thou shalt have no other gods before me" (Ex. 20:3). This is because all other gods are man-made. There is only one God who made man. He alone is the true God. "Remember the former things of old; for I am God, and there is none else; I am God, and there is none like me, declaring the end from the beginning, and from ancient times the things that are not yet done, saying, My counsel shall stand, and I will do all my pleasure" (Isa. 46:9–10). Without hesitation or apology God has placed within His resume that He alone is Creator and there is none like Him. "To whom, then, will ye liken me, or shall I be equal? saith the Holy One" (Isa. 40:25). "Is there a God beside me? Yea, there is no God; I know not any" (Isa.44:8c). It would seem man has become obsessed with "god making." Humanity has surrounded themselves with self-created gods, as many and varied as the cultures they come from. It would be easy to become frustrated in the search for the one true God, but "He" giveth more grace. The true God cannot be found apart from His grace.

No Carved Images

Commandment number two describes in detail what commandment number one means. "Thou shalt not make unto thee any carved image, or any likeness of anything that is in heaven above, or that is in the earth beneath, or that is in the water under the earth; Thou shalt not bow down thyself to them, nor serve them; for I, the Lord thy God, am a jealous God, visiting the iniquity of the fathers upon the children unto the third and fourth generation of them that hate me; and showing mercy unto thousands of them that love me, and keep my commandments" (Ex.20:4–6). There is only one God who made us, all other gods are our creations. "Know ye that the Lord, he is God; it is he who hath made us, and not we ourselves; we are his people, and the sheep of his pasture" (Psa. 100:3). In His resume He claims to have made all things including us, thus we are eating up His food, drinking up His water, breathing up His air, and taking up His space. I must confess at times I feel like an idolater because my heart is so quick to worship my creature needs and so slow to give thanks for my Creator's provisions. "Who exchanged the truth of God for a lie, and worshiped and served the creature more than the Creator, who is blessed forever. Amen" (Rom. 1:25). More often times than not to my shame, my favorite idol is the one that looks like me, thinks like me, and talks like me; namely, me.

THE RIGHT TO JUDGE

When man broke the rule not to eat of the forbidden tree, God had the right to judge. Not only did He have the right to judge but the need to judge. The law, when violated, must be accompanied with a penalty. Violators must face a judge who has the authority to enforce the law and hand down punishment or there is no law. God judged man when He cast him out of the beautiful garden He had created for him. He placed an angel with a flaming sword to make sure he wasn't able to return. God cursed the ground and told man he would have to make his living with the toil of his hands and by the sweat of his brow. There would be competitive thorns and thistles that would steal moisture and nutrients from the plants he was cultivating. His wife would have a near-death experience bearing children. He would have to fear harm or possible death from certain animals. All of creation, including man, would come under the bondage of corruption, begin to age and eventually die. God judged man's sin and all of creation bears evidence of this judgment. "For we know that the whole creation groaneth and travaileth in pain together until now. And not only they, but ourselves also, who have the first fruits of the Spirit, even we ourselves groan within ourselves, waiting for the adoption, that is, the redemption of our body" (Rom. 8:22–23).

THE JUDGMENT OF GOD

By Adam's disobedience he and his descendants received a sinful nature. That first act of sin brought death not only to his body in time, but also left his mind, will, and emotions immediately estranged from the rule of God. "Wherefore, as by one man sin entered into the world, and death by sin, and so death passed upon all men, for all have sinned" (Rom. 5:12). This is evidence of the righteous judgment of God upon sin. As Abraham said "Shall not the judge of all the earth do right?" (Gen. 18:25c)

Early in God's resume (by the way, He is not looking for a job) He shows us His righteous judgment and His grace. "And God saw that the wickedness of man was great in the earth, and that every imagination of the thoughts of his heart was only evil continually. And it repented the Lord that he had made man on the earth, and it grieved him at his heart. And the Lord said, I will destroy man whom I have created from the face of the earth; both man, and beast, and the creeping thing, and the fowls of the air; for it repenteth me that I have made them. BUT NOAH FOUND GRACE IN THE EYES OF THE LORD" (Gen. 6:5–8 emphasis mine). Noah was a preacher of the righteous judgment of God. He gave the men of his day warnings that God was going to judge the earth with a great flood and people needed to repent and prepare for this judgment. He faithfully obeyed God's instructions: built an ark, gathered the animals, and stocked it with the necessary provisions. Men all around him saw the boat but continued on with business as usual until the day they saw Noah get on the boat and God shut the door. After seven days of grace the judgment came upon the earth and only Noah and his family were saved. The judgment of God is not something to be toyed with. "For if God spared not the angels that sinned, but cast them down to hell, and delivered them into chains of darkness, to be reserved unto judgment; And spared not the old world, but saved Noah, the eighth person, a preacher of righteousness, bringing in the flood upon the world of the ungodly; And turning the cities of Sodom and Gomorrah into ashes, condemned them with an overthrow, making them an example unto those that after should live ungodly; And delivered just Lot, vexed with the filthy manner of life of the wicked, (For that righteous man dwelling among them, in seeing and hearing, vexed his righteous soul from day to day with their unlawful deeds), The Lord knoweth how to deliver the godly out of temptations, and to reserve the unjust unto the day of judgment to be punished" (2 Pet. 2:4–9).

God judged the land of Egypt in the days of Moses. He smote the firstborn of all who were not in a dwelling that had the prescribed blood on the lintel and the door post. "And it came to pass, that at midnight the Lord smote all the first-born in the land of Egypt, from the first-born of Pharaoh who sat on his throne unto the first-born of the captive who was in the dungeon; and all the firstborn of cattle. And Pharaoh rose up in the night, he, and all his servants, and all the Egyptians, and there was a great cry in Egypt; for there was not a house where there was not one dead" (Ex. 12:29–30). One or more in every house may seem severe, but were it not for grace all of Adam's race would have been destroyed; in fact Adam would have never had a race, it would have ended in the garden. He giveth more grace.

FUTURE JUDGMENT

Without understanding the cross of Christ I don't think I could bear the thought of future judgment of my sin. I tremble enough at the thought of standing before the judgment seat of Christ and having my works judged. God has made it clear that we must all give an account of ourselves before Him (see

Rom. 14:12). Every person, regardless of his belief system, would agree the one appointment we must all keep is our appointment with death. But there is more after that. "And as it is appointed unto men once to die, but after this the judgment" (Heb. 9:27). There is coming a day in which God will judge the entire world with His righteous judgment. "Because he hath appointed a day, in which he will judge the world in righteousness by that man whom he hath ordained; concerning which he hath given assurance unto all men, in that he hath raised him from the dead" (Acts 17:31). It is a fearful thing to fall into the hands of the living God. Yet, it is only the grace of God that enables us to fear the Judge and His righteous judgment of sin.

THE MEANING OF THE CROSS

Earlier I said if God did not create us, He has no right to rule us. If He has no right to rule us, He has no right to judge us, and if He has no right to judge us, the Cross is absolutely meaningless. The God of the Bible has made all three claims: He made us, has the right to rule us, and has the right to judge us. This being said gives the Cross of Christ the greatest meaning of any single event in history. When one understands the meaning of the Cross the only thing left to do is establish a relationship with God through faith in what He in His grace and mercy has done.

There are many prophesies in God's Word. Prophecy is history written in advance. In Psalms 22 David prophesied of the Cross in explicit detail a thousand years before its occurrence. It was written, before Rome was ever on the scene, let alone before crucifixion was its main means of execution. David saw the Cross of Christ would be God's righteous demonstration of

His judgment on man's sin. It would be Jesus Christ, the Just One paying the penalty for sinful unjust man.

Man needed justification with God yet we were helpless to justify ourselves under the uncompromising rules of God's law. Because of Adam's disobedience we were born in rebellion against God with a natural bent to live in opposition to His rule over us. The grace of God and the justice of God came together at the Cross when God gave His only begotten Son to be the sin bearer for man. One may ask how just is God? "He spared not his own Son, but delivered him up for us all" (Rom. 8:32a). God's standard of justice can only be reckoned by the gracious substitution of His sinless self in the person of His Son. This is the only acceptable sacrifice for man's sin. Because of what happened at the Cross we can be made just before a righteous judge. "For Christ also hath once suffered for sins, the just for the unjust, that he might bring us to God, being put to death in the flesh but made alive by the Spirit" (1 Pet. 3:18).

God's prophet Isaiah also wrote of the sufferings and death of Christ some 700 years prior to the event. He spoke about the hatred and rejection He would receive at the hands of man. The judgment of sin could be settled in no other way and in no other place than at the Cross. There and only there would the judgment of sinful man be placed on the sinless Son of God. "He is despised and rejected of men, a man of sorrows, and acquainted with grief, and we hid as it were our faces from him; he was despised, and we esteemed him not. Surely he hath borne our griefs, and carried our sorrows; yet we did esteem him stricken, smitten of God, and afflicted. But he was wounded for our transgressions, he was bruised for our iniquities; the chastisement for our peace was upon him, and with his stripes we are healed. All we like sheep have gone astray; we have turned every one to his own way, and the Lord hath laid on him the iniquity of us all" (Isa. 53:3–6). The cross of Christ is the judgment of God and the grace of God at its finest hour.

SOME BELIEVE AND SOME DON'T

God has made it very clear: there is no Plan B. There is no other way to be justified before the Righteous Judge than to be justified by faith in Christ and what He provided for us at the Cross. "To declare, I say, at this time his righteousness, that he might be just, and the justifier of him who believeth in Jesus" (Rom. 3:26).

There are other examples of justification by faith alone, but my favorite is the one that took place at the very cross itself. Jesus was crucified between two thieves. Both were with Him on the way to the crucifixion, both heard the accusations from the crowd, both heard the words of Jesus from the Cross, and eventually both saw Him die before their own deaths. Both initially mocked Him along with the crowd but one later repented and believed. The other never got his focus off the here and now and died an unbeliever. The first acknowledged they both were getting what justice demanded but that Jesus had done nothing to deserve what He was suffering. When one sees the truth of Jesus and the justice of God at the Cross, he will also see the grace of God at the Cross. The believing thief realized that nothing he had done in his past would disqualify him from the request he was about to make. He also realized there would be nothing he could do in the future that would merit or entitle him to make his request. There was certainly nothing he could do at the present to prevent what was about to happen. It was by the grace of God that he saw beyond that brief moment of this life. The grace of God showed him a future kingdom where Jesus was King and in simple faith he believed. "And he said unto Jesus, Lord, remember me when thou comest into thy kingdom. And Jesus said unto him, Verily I say unto thee, Today shalt thou be with me in paradise" (Lu. 23:42–43). This is the message of the gospel commanded to be preached in the entire world. It is the message of the grace of God at the cross. "For Christ sent me not to baptize but to preach the gospel; not with wisdom of words, lest the cross of Christ should be made of no effect. For the preaching of the cross is to them that perish foolishness; but unto us who are saved it is the power of God" (1 Cor. 1:17–18).

The apostle Paul faithfully preached the gospel message to both Jews and Gentiles. "And some believed the things which were spoken, and some believed not" (Acts 28:24). It is only by the grace of God anyone believes any of His story of Creation, Judgment, or Grace. And without hesitation or apology, I believe this is the "He" who giveth more grace.

CHAPTER TWO

WHAT GRACE IS THIS?

"I have written briefly, exhorting, and testifying that this is the true grace of God in which ye stand" (1 Pet. 5:12b). In the closing salutations of Peter's first letter he wanted to make clear that the things he had just written were in fact the true grace of God. In response to that statement one needs to ask the question, "Is it possible for there to be a false or counterfeit grace?" Is it possible for someone to take the true grace of God and corrupt its originally intended meaning and purpose? "For there are certain men crept in unawares, who were before of old ordained to this condemnation, ungodly men, turning the grace of our God into lasciviousness, and denying the only Lord God, and our Lord Jesus Christ" (Jude 4). When grace is preached as license to continue in the life of sin with no intention of repentance or a cry for help from God, this is false grace. True grace is the divine enabling power of God for me to do what God has called me to do. "And God is able to make all grace abound toward you, that ye, always having all suffi-ciency in all things, may abound to every good work" (2 Cor. 9:8). The grace of God does not claim to eradicate the old sinful nature but it does claim to bestow a greater power in the new or divine nature received when a person is born again.

The Two Natures

When the grace of God that brings salvation comes into the life of a person, they are born again. They now have two natures. There is the old nature which is prone to sin and still has the capacity for depraved behavior. It still has an aptitude for rebellion against God and His teachings. This is called the natural man or the old man. The new nature that is received from the Spirit of God is the one that wants to walk in the ways of God. This is called the new man or the spiritual man.

The Natural Man	The Spiritual Man
Born only of the flesh	Born of God
Powered by the law	Powered by grace
Produces self-righteousness	Produces true righteousness
Glorifies man	Glorifies God
Approved of by man	Approved of by God

One of the best proofs that a person is truly born again is evidence of the battle between the old nature and the new nature. These two natures will never agree on anything. "For the flesh lusteth against the Spirit, and the Spirit against the flesh; and these are contrary the one to the other, so that ye cannot do the things that ye would. But if ye be led by the Spirit, ye are not under the law. Now the works of the flesh are manifest, which are these: adultery, fornication, uncleanness, lasciviousness, idolatry, sorcery, hatred, strife, jealously, wrath, factions, seditions, heresies, envying's, murders, drunkenness, reveling, and the like; of which I tell you before, as I have also told you in time past, that they who do such things shall not inherit the kingdom of God. But the fruit of the Spirit is love, joy, peace, longsuffering, gentleness, goodness, faith, meekness, self-control; against such there is no law" (Gal. 5:17–23).

You can be a very religious person yet not be born again nor has the Spirit of God nor the new nature. You can be sincere in your desire to do things for God and keep His commandments, but if at the heart of your desires there is not an absolute dependence on the grace of God and what He has accomplished for you at the cross, then you have missed the gospel. You need to repent and put your complete confidence in what He has done for you, not in what you do for God. At the cross God judged our sin in the person of His Son Jesus Christ. This and this alone is the foundation for a faith relationship with God. Without understanding and embracing the Cross, it would be impossible for a believer to understand the battle that goes on in his life and his need for the grace of God to follow Christ. It is so important for us to have a good understanding of the gospel. We need to preach it to ourselves and hear it often from others who are like minded until we become established in the faith. "As ye have, therefore, received Christ Jesus the Lord, so walk ye in him, rooted and built up in him, and established in the faith, as ye have been taught, abounding with thanksgiving" (Col. 2:6–7). In the upcoming chapter on grace for sanctification we will deal more thoroughly on ways to help us become established in the faith.

SOME PEOPLE NEED GRACE AND SOME DON'T

I chose the title for this book from James 4:6, BUT HE GIVETH MORE GRACE. All of the translations end that phrase with a period. It is a complete sentence, which speaks volumes about the grace of God. But the rest of the verse continues with these words, "Wherefore he saith, God resisteth the proud, but giveth grace unto the humble". The reason God doesn't give grace to the proud is because they don't need it. The proud man is more than able to pull off life without help from the God who made him. The proud man sees all things, understands all things, is capable of all things and doesn't need any help from anyone, least of all God. Oh, the pride of life, when a man thinks himself to be something when he is nothing, he deceives himself. Is there ever a sin more prominent, more persistent than the sin of human pride? Pride hunts and haunts both Christian and non-Christian alike pursuing him to the very brink of eternity. Bringing pride and grace together are like trying to put together similar poles of magnets, they oppose each other. God resisteth the proud. It is indeed a wonder that any of us have found grace in His sight. By the way, even the proud man needs grace; he just doesn't see it that way. Thank you, Lord, that You have included graciousness in Your Holy nature regardless of our sinful pride.

On the other hand the people who need God's divine enabling power for life are the humble. The humble man recognizes his deficit in every column of life temporal and eternal. The humble man acknowledges his absolute dependence on the God who made him and knows what is best for him. The humble man sees God as the sovereign Lord of the universe who condescended to men of low estate to bring him eternal salvation through faith in the gospel. When the grace of God that brings salvation appears to a man and he responds in humble faith, God lifts him up. When the worst of sinners humble themselves, God gives them grace. "Two men went up into the temple to pray; the one a Pharisee, and the other a tax collector. The Pharisee stood and prayed thus with himself, God I thank thee that I am not as other men are, extortioners, unjust, adulterers, or even as this tax collector. I fast twice in the week; I give tithes of all that I possess. And the tax collector, standing afar off, would not lift up so much as his eyes unto heaven, but smote upon his breast, saying, God be merciful to me a sinner. I tell you, this man went down to his house justified rather than the other; for everyone that exalteth himself shall be abased; and he that humbleth himself shall be exalted" (Luke. 18:10–14).

THE MYSTERY OF GRACE

Since all men have within their nature only the tendency to be proud how do they humble themselves? Is it that men have a capacity within themselves to become humble so they can receive more grace? If so, then man would have some capacity within himself to produce righteousness apart from the grace of God. The Lord makes this very clear through the pen of the Apostle Paul, as well as others. "As it is written, There is none righteous, no, not one; There is none that understandeth, there is none that seeketh after God. They are all gone out of the way, they are together become unprofitable; there is none that doeth good, no, not one" (Rom. 3:10–12). When a man humbles himself before God, puts his faith in the grace of Christ and His substitutionary work at the Cross, he is born again. It is all credited to the grace of God. When a man hears the Word of His grace (the gospel), the Spirit of grace does the work of conviction, revelation, and yes, even repentance and faith. All these workings make a man response-able, or able to respond. "For by grace are ye saved through faith; and that not of yourselves, it is the gift of God—not of works, lest any man should boast" (Eph. 2:8–9). All men who are saved are saved by grace through faith; but not all men who hear the gospel are convicted of sin and have the Spirit reveal the truth, respond and are saved. By the grace of God I did understand the gospel of salvation, but to this day I still don't know all the particulars of salvation by grace. Yet I know when a person enters heaven God isn't surprised by their arrival. He instead declares that He knew their response from before the foundations of the world. God does the choosing, yet He has given man a choice. Either of these truths taken to the extreme soon become heresy; lend themselves to confusion and unnecessary division. I cannot place these truths in a neat little system of theology, but instead I have become content not to objectify mystery. This book is not an attempt to resolve that issue but hopefully will stay focused on "He" giveth more grace.

Appreciating What You Know

It seems the more I learn, the more there is to learn. Rather than become discouraged with all I have yet to learn I find grace to appreciate what I have learned. By the grace of God I plan on being a student until He calls me home. My heart resonates with the words of the Apostle Paul to the church at Corinth, "For we know in part, and we prophecy in part. ... For now we see in a mirror darkly; but then, face to face; now I know in part, but then shall I know even as also I am known" (1 Cor. 13:9, 12). I feel as if I am writing on a subject that I am looking at through a welder's mask. I may not always see it as clearly as someone else, but occasionally there is an arc and I catch a glimpse of truth.

One of the glimpses that God in His grace has given me is in reference to the law and sin. As our culture moves farther and farther from "all men are CREATED equal" to our origin found somewhere in the evolutionary process of time, we don't like to hear the word "sin". The word "sin" so accurately smacks of law breakers. Maybe the problem is the law. Maybe if we got rid of the law we could get rid of sin. The truth is we can't get rid of sin any more than we can get rid of the law. We can't get rid of the law any more than we can get rid of the law-giver. Trying to get rid of the law-giver is the same as trying to get rid of the Creator. The Creator was here before the world began and He will be around when this old world is judged and all things are made new.

THE LAW AND SIN

"For the law was given by Moses, but grace and truth came by Jesus Christ" (John 1:17). God did not give Moses the Ten Commandments in order to *establish* a relationship with His people, but to *confirm* a relationship with His people. You don't make rules for other peoples' kids. The Law was given to point out several truths:

⬦ We know what sin is and know we are sinners. "Therefore, by the deeds of the law there shall no flesh be justified in his sight; for by the law is the knowledge of sin" (Rom. 3:20).

⬦ The more laws, the more obvious man's failure to keep them. "Moreover, the law entered, that the offense might abound" (Rom. 5:20a).

⬦ The harder I try to keep the Law, the worse I do. "Was then that which is good made death unto me? God forbid. But sin, that it might appear sin, working death in me by that which is good—that sin by the commandment might become exceedingly sinful. For we know that the law is spiritual; but I am carnal, sold under sin" (Rom. 7:13–14). We know that we are born under the Law, we can't escape it, and nothing reveals my moral bankruptcy quicker than the Law. This Law is written by God on every man's heart regardless of his culture.

✧ The Law is a schoolmaster who points us to Christ. "Wherefore, the law was our schoolmaster to bring us unto Christ, that we might be justified by faith. But after faith is come, we are no longer under a schoolmaster. For ye are all the sons of God by faith in Christ Jesus" (Gal. 3:24–26).

I have tried justification by the commandment route. Even now in short lived moments of stupidity I pay a return visit to that path. A visit may be alright as a reminder of its impossibility, but only a fool thinks he can maintain it as his permanent residence. Trying to keep the rules in order to maintain my peace with God only led me to condemnation, deception, and death. Oh, the problem wasn't with the Law or the Law-Maker but with my ability to keep the rules. His standard of perfection is beyond my reach and try as I might I cannot attain unto it. "Oh, wretched man that I am! Who shall deliver me from the body of this death? I thank God through Jesus Christ, our Lord. So, then, with the mind I myself serve the law of God; but with the flesh, the law of sin. There is, therefore, now no condemnation to them who are in Christ Jesus" (Rom. 7:24–8:1a). The Law demands perfection and only grace meets that demand.

Amazing grace, how sweet the sound,
that saved a wretch like me.

I once was lost but now am found,
was blind, but now I see.
    John Newton

"Christ hath redeemed us from the curse of the law, being made a curse for us; for it is written, Cursed is everyone that hangeth on a tree; That the blessing of Abraham might come on the Gentiles through Jesus Christ, that we might receive the promise of the Spirit through faith"(Gal. 3:13–14). I feel like shouting all over again. Every time I go back to the Law I get worn out under its heavy burden. But when I take His yoke, I find rest to my soul. The yoke of Jesus is easy and His burden is light and I will tell you why: "For the law was given by Moses, but grace and truth came by Jesus Christ" (John 1:17).

Wonderful grace of Jesus, greater than all my sin;
How shall my tongue describe it?
Where shall its praise begin?
Taking away my burden, setting my spirit free,
For the wonderful grace of Jesus reaches me.
    Haldor Lillenas

I am going to take a little break from writing and spend some time in worship.

THE NEED FOR SOUND DOCTRINE

"Beloved, when I gave all diligence to write to unto you of the common salvation, it was needful for me to write unto you, and exhort you that you should earnestly contend for the faith which was once delivered unto the saints. For there are certain men crept in unawares, who were before of old ordained to this condemnation, ungodly men, turning the grace of our God into lasciviousness, and denying the only Lord God, and our Lord Jesus Christ" (Jude 3–4). There is no doubt about the power of sin. The ravages of its power are evident everywhere. As believers we know that the power of grace is greater than the power of sin. "But where sin abounded, grace did much more abound" (Rom. 5:20b). The power of the Cross and the empty tomb speak volumes of the power of God's grace in overcoming sin. Sound Biblical teaching helps us know what true grace is all about. We must strive to know the Biblical doctrines and pursue them as close as we possibly can. We must fight the temptation to adjust our theology to accommodate our sin. The church throughout the ages has faced this issue and faces it still today. False grace will always produce false doctrines that depart from the faith that was once delivered to the saints.

One of the hallmarks of the early church was: "And they continued steadfastly in the apostles' doctrine and fellowship, and in breaking of bread, and in prayers" (Acts. 2:42). As the church spread throughout the world the apostles gave warnings of false prophets and false doctrines. "But there were false prophets also among the people, even as there shall be false teachers among you, who secretly shall bring in destructive heresies, even denying the Lord that bought them, and bring upon themselves swift destruction. And many shall follow their pernicious ways, by reason of whom the truth shall be evil spoken of" (2 Pet. 2:1–2). The apostles knew if the Church was to grow up in Christ they would need to become established in the basic doctrines of the Word of God. If sound doctrine disappeared they would be left to the false teachers that trot alongside the flock like a pack of wolves lying in wait to deceive.

When a person loses their stability in the gospel they also lose the power to accurately and effectively proclaim it. "That we henceforth be no more children, tossed to and fro, and carried about with every wind of doctrine, by the sleight of men, and cunning craftiness, by which they lie in wait to deceive" (Eph. 4:14). Not always, but usually people can tell if someone has lost their footing and if they really believe what they're saying.

Sound doctrine makes the Christian strong in true grace. False doctrine makes men strong in false grace. False doctrine leads men in directions they never dreamed they would go and leaves them in places they never dreamed they'd be found. "Preach the word; be diligent in season, out of season; reprove, rebuke, exhort with all longsuffering and doctrine. For the time will come when they will not endure sound doctrine but, after their own lusts, shall they heap to themselves teachers, having itching ears; and they shall turn away their ears from the truth, and shall be turned unto fables" (2 Tim. 4:2–4). False teaching was of grave concern to the apostles because they knew that in the latter times some would depart from the faith. "Now the Spirit speaketh expressly that, in the latter times, some shall depart from the faith, giving heed to seducing spirits, and doctrines of demons, speaking lies in hypocrisy, having their conscience seared with a hot iron" (1 Tim. 4:1–2). When many who were strong in their faith in Christ abandon it, we will know that the last days are drawing to a close. "Let no man deceive you by any means; for that day shall not come, except there come the falling away first, and that man of sin be revealed, the son of perdition" (2 Thes. 2:3). The words "falling away" are from the Greek word *apostasia* which means turning away, rebellion or abandonment. This will occur in greater degrees as Christians abandon basic Bible doctrine.

THREE RELEVANT EXAMPLES
OF SOUND DOCTRINE

#1. Creation—Since the publication of Darwin's theory of evolution, <u>The Origin of Species</u> in 1859 there has been increasing pressure to accept the theory as scientific fact. In 1968, the U.S. Supreme Court ruled that evolution was the only option to be taught in the public school sector leaving the origin of life just a series of accidents. If we do not believe in a Biblically described, God-created origin, then we have no foundation for a Biblically described destiny. We have no basis for a God-created meaning or purpose. If we are here as a result of 3½ billion years of evolution, it would seem our only purpose is to be born, live a few short years in which we reproduce and then die. The meaning and purpose of life would be reduced to propagation of the species left only to mindlessly repeating the process until we evolve into something else. We should be insulted by such insanity. God in His pleasure created all things for His glory and honor. He has made a way for us to find the highest meaning of life which is to honor and worship Him with a life of gratefulness. "Thou art worthy, O Lord, to receive glory and honor and power; for thou hast created all things, and for thy pleasure they are and were created" (Rev. 4:11).

#2. Marriage—God created marriage as it is recorded in the second chapter of Genesis. This was before any mention of the Ten Commandments or the Church (which is a picture of Christ and His bride). The truth of marriage was to be foundational to everything in creation. "Therefore shall a man leave his father and his mother, and shall cleave unto his wife; and they shall be one flesh" (Gen. 2:24). One man and one woman, not man with man or woman with woman.

We now live in a culture that endorses same sex marriage and has tried to legalize what God has declared a violation of His divine design and law. If the church concedes this fundamental doctrine, where will it end? The church cannot rise above the caliber of the families which form it. As the family goes, so goes the church; as the church goes, so goes the nation. Even without the church's salt and light marriage and family are still the basic units of any culture or society. When marriage and family begin to deteriorate it won't be long before the entire culture unravels. When we trade this truth for a lie we accelerate the decline of our nation.

"Who exchanged the truth of God for a lie, and worshiped and served the creature more than the Creator, who is blessed forever. Amen. For this cause God gave them up unto vile affections; for even their women did exchange the natural use for that which is against nature; And likewise also the men, leaving the natural use of the woman, burned in their lust one toward another, men with men working that which is unseemly, and receiving in themselves that recompense of their error which was fitting. And even as they did not like to retain God in their knowledge, God gave them over to a reprobate mind, to do those things which are not seemly" (Rom. 1:25–28). A reprobate mind is a dangerous thing; it's a mind which no longer has the ability to process truth. "Woe unto them who call evil, good, and good, evil; who put darkness for light, and light for darkness; who put bitter for sweet, and sweet for bitter! Woe unto them who are wise in their own eyes, and prudent in their own sight!" (Isa. 5:20–21).This is nothing new; the prophets of Jeremiah's day made similar compromises and the nation of Israel followed a similar path before God judged them and removed them from the land. "An appalling and horrible thing is committed in the land; The prophets prophesy falsely, and the priests bear rule by their means, and my people love to have it so; and what will ye do in the end of it all?" (Jer. 5:30–31).

Let me say that since the fall of man, it is in man's nature to be a law breaker. Every man has the potential for homosexuality as they have the capacity to violate this Law and every other Law of God. It is only by the grace of God we can deal with our lawlessness. The curse of sin is more sin. The blessing of grace is more grace. But "He", the Creator, Rule Maker, and Judge is able to give us more grace. Where sin abounded, grace did much more abound. This is sound doctrine! In contrast the doctrine of evolution is consistent in claiming that homosexuality is a genetic tendency and nothing can or should be done about it. If that view is true, where does it end? What human behavior, regardless of how vile it is, cannot be blamed on some stage of my evolutionary development? Regenerating grace opposes this false doctrine. If man is ever to deal successfully with this or any other sin he must do it through the sanctifying grace of God.

#3. Judgment to come—The book of Acts records the violent reaction of the Jews against the Apostle Paul's preaching of the gospel. The mob in Jerusalem would have torn him to pieces if the Roman soldiers had not rescued him. Paul was eventually removed to Caesarea and placed under the protection of Felix the Roman procurator over Judea. When Paul was given the opportunity to defend himself he cut to the chase and made known that the charges against him were largely because of his faith in the resurrection of the dead. "Except it be for this one thing, that I cried standing among them, concerning the resurrection of the dead I am called in question by you this day" (Acts 24:21). Felix adjourned the trial and postponed his ruling until a later date. The accusers were dismissed and Paul was called in for a private hearing with Felix and his wife, Drusilla, who was a Jewess. As was Paul's custom, he reasoned with him of self-righteousness versus the imputed righteousness of the gospel. He reasoned with him of self-control, as well control of self by the Holy Spirit. He reasoned with him of his need to present a flawless case before God under the law. Felix being a judge understood all too well what it meant to judge people according to law and trembled at the thought of someday standing before the great Judge and giving account of his life according to the laws of heaven. "And as he reasoned of righteousness, self-control, and judgment to come, Felix trembled, and answered, Go thy way for this time; when I have a convenient season, I will call for thee" (Acts 24:25).

True doctrines of grace cannot forfeit the vital teaching of judgment to come. God alone has the right and responsibility to judge individuals and nations, the redeemed as well as those who have gone their own way, even the living and the dead. "I charge thee, therefore, before God, and the Lord Jesus Christ, who shall judge the living and the dead at his appearing and his kingdom" (2 Tim. 4:1). "So, then, every one of us shall give account of himself to God" (Rom. 14:12). It is the goodness of God when we are warned of judgment to come. Many a man has responded to this warning by seeking the mercy and grace of God, repented from their unbelief and trusted Christ for their hope of eternal life. The reality of judgment is as sure as the reality of death. Only faith in the grace of Christ will keep us from perishing in the judgment and condemnation of our sin that is sure to come. "For God so loved the world, that he gave his only begotten Son, that whosoever believeth in him should not perish, but have eternal life. For God sent not his

Son into the world to condemn the world, but that the world through him might be saved. He that believeth on him is not condemned; but he that believeth not is condemned already, because he hath not believed in the name of the only begotten Son of God. And this is the condemnation, that light is come into the world, and men loved darkness rather than light, because their deeds were evil. For everyone that doeth evil hateth the light, neither cometh to the light, lest his deeds should be reproved. But he that doeth truth cometh to the light, that his deeds may be made manifest, that they are wrought in God" (John 3:16–21). God is gracious in telling us in advance of the judgment to come and of the judgment already handed out to Christ at the cross for our sakes. In faith turn to Christ now, ask Him for mercy, ask Him to forgive your trespasses and receive the gift of salvation. It is the only way to be justified before the Judge. "Being justified freely by his grace through the redemption that is in Christ Jesus" (Rom. 3:24). If you are by grace response-able, don't delay, trust Christ today.

CHAPTER THREE

GRACE FOR SALVATION

O n occasion, after preaching the gospel by speaking of "salvation" or by encouraging the lost to be "saved", someone will inquire, "What is a person "saved" from?" My standard response is: God. I am saved from the righteous judgment of a holy God against my sin. I was born a rebel, opposed to His authority as the Maker and Ruler of my life. By grace through faith He led me to repentance from my rebellion and saved me from the penalty and power of unbelief. At that moment my identity before God changed: from condemned to justified; from guilty to forgiven; from headed to hell to seated in heavenly places in Christ Jesus; from lost to found, from blind to seeing, from captivity to freedom. I am saved from the judgment of what I deserve, to all the blessings of eternity that I do not deserve. Were it not for the grace of God I would still be wandering in darkness and my hope of salvation would be left up to my own devices.

QUALITY CONTROL

The quality of righteousness that God demands for my salvation is not something I could produce on my best day. I will say this as plainly as I can: my righteousness has nothing to do with my eternal salvation. What a blessing it is when a person understands this simple, yet profound truth. It's not hard to love the Savior when you realize you are justified freely by His grace. "Being justified freely by his grace through the redemption that is in Christ Jesus" (Rom. 3:24). My justification has nothing to do with my own personal righteousness. "Not by works of righteousness which we have done, but according to his mercy he saved us, by the washing of regeneration, and renewing of the Holy Spirit, which he shed on us abundantly through Jesus Christ, our Savior, that being justified by his grace, we should be made heirs according to the hope of eternal life" (Titus 3:5–7).

Man would be helpless and forever lost if his hope of heaven was dependent on his ability to produce God's standard of righteousness. Even the children of Israel, God's chosen people, were not chosen because of any self-righteousness. "Not for thy righteousness, nor for the uprightness of thine heart, dost thou go to possess their land, but for the wickedness of these nations the Lord thy God doth drive them out from before thee, and that he may perform the word which the Lord swore unto thy fathers, Abraham, Isaac, and Jacob. Understand, therefore, that the Lord thy God giveth thee not this good land to possess for thy righteousness: for thou art a stiff-necked people. Remember, and forget not, how thou provokedst the Lord thy God to wrath in the wilderness; from the day that thou didst depart out of the land of Egypt, until ye came unto this place, ye have been rebellious against the Lord" (Deut. 9:5–7).

It is truly the grace of God that brings salvation to the soul of man. What a gift of divine grace when a man truly understands the Word of God that describes the worthlessness of self-righteousness, when he comes under the convicting power of the Holy Spirit and understands that there is none righteous, no not one. "But we are all as an unclean thing, and all our righteousnesses are as filthy rags; and we all do fade as a leaf, and our iniquities, like the wind, have taken us away" (Isa. 64:6). When by grace God commands the light to shine out of darkness, we are able to first see our need of Christ and His righteousness then we declare Him as our Savior and Lord. "To declare, I say, at this time his righteousness, that he might be just, and the justifier of him who believeth in Jesus" (Rom. 3:26). This is the only salvation God offers. This salvation glorifies God and God alone. When God made His Son to become sin for us that we might be made the righteousness of God in Him, nobody but God is glorified. "That no flesh should glory in his presence. But of him are ye in Christ Jesus, who of God is made unto us wisdom, and righteousness, and sanctification, and redemption; That, according as it is written, He that glorieth, let him glory in the Lord" (1 Cor. 1:29–31).

GRACE AND ALL MEN

"For the grace of God that bringeth salvation hath appeared to all men" (Titus 2:11). Who qualifies for the grace of God? If it is the true grace of God we are talking about, nobody qualifies. If we are asking, "Is there some human merit that makes one eligible?" The answer is no. On the other hand, all men qualify for the grace of God. Truly the grace of God is available to all. Yes, all men— young and old, male and female educated or illiterate, strong and weak— for the grace of God that bringeth salvation has appeared to all men. Regardless of nationality, class, or creed, the call is to all men everywhere to repent and believe the gospel of grace, to turn from our dead works and serve the living God. The doctrine of grace and salvation through the gospel is for all classifications of men from the upper echelon to men of low estate, from men of high moral character to the vilest criminal.

Those who have been saved by grace through faith are commanded to take this message to the world and preach it with the understanding that all men are eligible for salvation. "For God so loved the world, that he gave his only begotten Son, that whosoever believeth in him should not perish, but have everlasting life" (John 3:16). We are to pray for the salvation of all men. We are not to look at anyone as unreachable by the grace of God. "I exhort, therefore, that first of all, supplications, prayers, intercessions, and giving of thanks, be made for all men, for kings, and for all that are in authority, that we may lead a quiet and peaceable life in all godliness and honesty. For this is good and acceptable in the sight of God, our Savior, who will have all men to be saved, and to come unto the knowledge of the truth. For there is one God, and one mediator between God and men, the man Christ Jesus, Who gave himself a ransom for all, to be testified in due time. For this I am ordained a preacher, and an apostle (I speak the truth in Christ, and lie not), a teacher of the Gentiles in faith and verity. I will, therefore, that men pray everywhere, lifting up holy hands, without wrath and doubting" (1 Tim. 2:1–8).

NO RESPECTOR OF PERSONS

The early church was Jewish. It was born in Jerusalem during the Feast of Pentecost also called the Feast of Weeks, or the Feast of Harvest. As the disciples were praying and waiting for the promise of the Holy Spirit, sure enough, He came and filled each believer present. His coming was like the sound of a mighty rushing wind and the disciples, now the church, took to the streets and spoke as the Spirit gave them utterance. In languages they had not learned, they proclaimed the wonderful works of God to devout Jews who had come from every nation under heaven. Yes the gospel of grace came to the Jews in Jerusalem first but it was meant for all people throughout the world. "But ye shall receive power, after the Holy Spirit is come upon you; and ye shall be witnesses unto me both in Jerusalem, and in all Judea, and in Samaria, and unto the uttermost part of the earth" (Acts 1:8).

In Acts 8 it is recorded that severe persecution came to the Jerusalem church and people scattered and wherever they went they preached the word of grace. Philip began an evangelistic ministry in Samaria and the church was officially on the move in obedience to the Lord's command. He shared the gospel with an Ethiopian man, he believed and was baptized. The powerful message of the gospel was going global, to all nations, as it was promised to Abraham.

In Acts 10 the account of Cornelius' conversion is recorded. Cornelius was a Roman centurion, a captain of 100 Roman soldiers, in a land where the Romans were unpopular and even despised by many. God spoke to the apostle Peter in three similar visions instructing him to remove his bigotry against the Gentiles and share with them the good news of the gospel of Christ. Reluctantly, Peter obeyed God and made the trip to the house of Cornelius. After a lengthy explanation of all the cultural and religious hurdles he had to cross in his feeble attempt to be obedient, Peter began his message. His opening statement is a giant step of growth in his understanding of the grace of his Lord Jesus Christ. "Then Peter opened his mouth, and said, Of a truth I perceive that God is no respecter of persons" (Acts 10:34).

James made it clear that followers of the Lord should not have respect of persons either. "My brethren, have not the faith of our Lord Jesus Christ, the Lord of glory, with respect of persons. For if there come unto your assembly a man with a gold ring, in fine apparel, and there come in also a poor man in vile raiment, And ye have respect to him that weareth the fine clothing, and say unto him, Sit thou here in a good place; and say to the poor, Stand thou there, or sit thou here under my footstool, Are ye not then partial in yourselves, and are become judges with evil thoughts" (Jas. 2:1–4).

GRACE THAT ENABLES MEN TO BELIEVE

I have a fear of oversimplifying what I am about to say and yet I have a greater fear of complicating it. It is difficult to keep simplicity from being complicated. "But I fear, lest by any means, as the serpent beguiled Eve through his craftiness, so your minds should be corrupted from the simplicity that is in Christ" (2 Cor. 11:3). Let me say that I do not know how to relieve the tension that exists between the sovereignty of God and the free will of man in salvation. I personally believe that I was free to choose the destiny unto which I was appointed before the foundation of the world. God was not shocked when I trusted Christ as my Savior; others may have been, but He was not.

There is an inseparable relationship between hearing the gospel and believing the gospel. It's possible to hear and not believe but it is not possible to believe the gospel without hearing it. "And some believed the things which were spoken, and some believed not" (Acts 28:24). Christians should never withhold sharing the gospel with anyone in any people group, regardless of their ethnic, religious, social or political position, for it is the power of God unto salvation to everyone that believeth. We should not fear sharing the gospel with someone who, in our weak evaluation, may not be able to believe it. It is only by the divine enabling power of His grace that anyone is able to believe the gospel. Yet it is through sharing the gospel of grace that God leads men to call on the name of the Lord and be saved. It is through hearing the gospel of grace that men believe on Christ as their only hope of eternal life. Few people, if any, understand the dynamics of grace that are going on at the moment of salvation. For that matter few people, if any, understand the dynamics of growing in grace even when they have been drenched with it their entire life.

PERSUADING GRACE

"Knowing, therefore, the terror of the Lord, we persuade men" (2 Cor. 5:11a). The thought of standing before God is both convicting and inspiring: convicting in that it should lead us to be diligent in godly living and inspiring in that we should do all we can to persuade men of the truth of the gospel. The Apostle Paul is an excellent example of a man fully persuaded by the grace of God. His faith is so wonderfully and accurately evidenced in his desire to persuade others. Paul began his ministry in Asia by going first to the synagogue in Ephesus and spending three months disputing and persuading the people concerning the kingdom of God. When the Jews hardened their hearts and began to speak evil of "the way", Paul took advantage of an opportunity to teach in the school of Tyrannus. We know little about this place other than that it became a launching pad for all Asia to hear the gospel. Paul saw it as his responsibility to persevere when attempting to persuade men of the gospel.

Paul gave a powerful and persuasive testimony of the grace of Christ before King Agrippa and his entourage of political dignitaries as is evidenced by Agrippa's response, "Almost thou persuadest me to be a Christian" (Acts 26:28b). Paul, recognizing the grace being given to Agrippa, wasted no time in pleading with him to trust the same Christ Paul himself had trusted. "And Paul said, I would to God that not only thou but also all that hear me this day were both almost , and altogether, such as I am, except these bonds" (Acts 26:29). Whether Paul was on the streets, in jail, or under house arrest in Rome, everywhere it was the same: he was trying to persuade men to believe the truth of the gospel.

FOR THE GOSPEL'S SAKE

Paul knew that he was free from all men, yet he became a servant to all men, in his passion to win more souls to Christ. To the Jew, he became a Jew, to the Gentile, he became a Gentile; to the weak he became weak that he might gain the weak. "I am made all things to all men, that I might by all means save some" (1 Cor. 9:22b). Paul did all of this for the gospel's sake. Paul saw the gospel as the very heart of God and persuading grace as a way he could work together with God. His persuasion escalated when he thought of man's natural desire to procrastinate and put off grace for another day. He pleaded with people not to receive the grace of God in vain, but to act immediately when God was calling them to salvation. "We, then, as workers together with him, beseech you also that ye receive not the grace of God in vain (For he saith, I have heard thee in a time accepted, and in the day of salvation have I helped thee; behold, now is the accepted time; behold, now is the day of salvation)" (2 Cor. 6:1–2). Self-examination quickly reveals (to my shame) that I am not as consistent in my passion for sharing the gospel as I ought to be but at this moment, I want to be as persuasive as I can: I encourage you to trust in the Lord today as opposed to a tomorrow that may never come.

CHAPTER FOUR

GRACE FOR SANCTIFICATION

Sanctification has its beginning when a person becomes a Christian. In the positional sense he is completely sanctified as he is completely justified by the redemptive work of Christ. A Christian's standing in grace is the result of the work of Christ alone. At the moment Christ is received by faith, regardless of how weak or ignorant the believer may be, he enters into the same position with Christ as the most illustrious saint. He is justified, sanctified, and glorified on the merits of Christ alone. You don't "do" justification; you are declared justified by faith in Christ. "Therefore, being justified by faith, we have peace with God through our Lord Jesus Christ" (Rom. 5:1). Should I live to be a hundred, I will never be more justified than I was the day I received Christ as my Savior. Sanctification on the other hand has a twofold provision.

A TWOFOLD PROVISION

Sanctification carries with it not only the positional standing but also the progressive transformation of a believer's life and

53

character into the image of Christ. It is bringing my behavior in line with my new identity as a Christian. It is following the command of Christ to be as holy in my conduct, conversation, and character as He already states I am. When a person receives Christ he is sealed by the Holy Spirit unto the day of redemption. He is also indwelt by the Holy Spirit who makes real for him a life conformed to the image of Christ. In a sense it is a gift as is every part of salvation, but it must be daily appropriated through a life of surrender to the will and ways of God found in His Word. It is best described in the benediction of Peter's second letter. "But grow in grace, and in the knowledge of our Lord and Savior, Jesus Christ. To him be glory both now and forever. Amen" (2 Pet. 3:18). Growing in grace is a lifelong process completed only when we see Christ.

The Epistles are constantly illustrating the distinction between the believers standing in Christ and his walk. My walk does not earn my standing! My standing before God is in the finished work of Christ alone! I am a recipient of this standing by grace through faith. In progressive sanctification I am a participant. When it comes to growing in grace I have responsibility to put off the old man and put on the new, to deny myself, take up my cross, and follow Christ. The grace of God makes me response-able. This divine ability does not make following Christ a cake walk but it does make it possible. It is the means by which believers grow into a strong personal faith and love for Christ. For years I have realized the Christian life preaches and teaches easier than it lives out. If the Christian life were easy more people would be living it. The simple truth is: it is absolutely impossible to live without dependence on Christ and His grace. It was never God's intention for us to live independent from Him or His provision for life. We were called by the grace of Christ to eternal salvation and we are called by the grace of Christ to work out our salvation. Without grace I could not have obeyed the call for salvation and without grace I cannot obey the call to sanctification. It's all grace from beginning to end. "As ye have, therefore, received Christ Jesus the Lord, so walk ye in him, rooted and built up in him, and established in the faith, as ye have been taught, abounding with thanksgiving" (Col. 2:6–7). I received Christ by grace through faith and I must walk with Him by grace through faith.

THE HEART OF SANCTIFICATION

The heart of man is referred to in Scripture more than 900 times and is almost never used in the literal sense of the organ that pumps blood throughout our body. Commonly, the heart is referred to as the seat of the intellect, emotions, and will, but most often it signifies the innermost part of our being. A man can lip-sync a sinner's prayer and be as lost as before he prayed. If a man's heart is not involved in faith, all the praying in the world will not save him. "For with the heart man believeth unto righteousness; and with the mouth confession is made unto salvation" (Rom. 10:10). The same is true of progressive sanctification. The heart must be involved. "But sanctify the Lord God in your hearts, and be ready always to give and answer to every man that asketh you a reason of the hope that is in you, with meekness and fear" (1 Pet. 3:15). One of the best evidences that someone is born again is the desire to follow Christ. When the Holy Spirit comes into a person's life he brings with him a desire to live a life of obedience to God. A new nature is planted in their soul and a new way of life is desired. As a newborn infant desires milk so he can live and grow up, so also does the newborn believer in Christ desire God's Word. The very Word of God that gave him life and salvation is the word he now desires to grow up in Christ. "Being born again, not of corruptible seed, but of incorruptible, by the word of God, which liveth and abideth forever" (1 Pet. 1:23). "As newborn babes, desire the pure milk of the word, that ye may grow by it" (1 Pet. 2:2).

A New Way of Living

Solomon was a man who at one time walked in the ways of the Lord. He supervised the building of the temple in Jerusalem and then dedicated it to the Lord. The presence of the Lord was made obvious to the people and true worship occurred. As time went on however, Solomon wandered away from the Lord and near the end of his life he penned the book of Ecclesiastes. This book records the pessimistic words of a cynical old man who has walked away from God. "The thing that hath been, it is that which shall be; and that which is done, is that which shall be done; and there is no new thing under the sun" (Eccl. 1:9). The wisest of men left to human reasoning alone will come to the same conclusion: life is vanity and vexation of spirit. When men walk in the ways of God though, "New" is stamped all over it.

King David knew of both the old way and the new way of living. "I waited patiently for the Lord, and he inclined unto me, and heard my cry. He brought me up also out of an horrible pit, out of the miry clay, and set my feet upon a rock, and established my goings. And he hath put a *new* song in my mouth, even praise unto our God; many shall see it, and fear, and shall trust in the Lord. Blessed is the man who maketh the Lord his trust, and respecteth not the proud, nor such as turn aside to lies" (Psa. 40:1–3).

Jeremiah the prophet knew of the new way of living. God had pleaded with Israel to return to Him and walk in His ways. The prophets had warned of impending chastisement and judgment. Jeremiah had witnessed the fall of Jerusalem and the destruction of the temple. As he looked around he couldn't help but weep for the people of God and what had become of them. As he considered all that had happened, he penned these words: "It is because of the Lord's mercies that we are not consumed, because his compassions fail not. They are *new* every morning; great is thy faithfulness. The Lord is my portion, saith my soul; therefore will I hope in him. The Lord is good unto those who wait for him, to the soul that seeketh him. It is good that a man should both hope and quietly wait for the salvation of the Lord" (Lam. 3:22–26). Even in the midst of chastisement Jeremiah understood that God's faithfulness and mercy to Israel would return them to their former glory through Christ. "Behold, the days come, saith the Lord, that I will make a new covenant with the house of Israel, and with the house of Judah" (Jer. 31:31). Jesus is the Lion of the tribe of Judah and the Eternal Living Word of God Who would become flesh and save His people from their sins. This word was in Jeremiah's heart like a burning coal of fire and would not go out regardless of the severe judgment of God on sin.

When a person is born again he becomes a new creation. "Therefore, if any man be in Christ, he is a *new* creation; old things are passed away; behold, all things are become *new*" (2 Cor. 5:17). He has been taken from where he was dead in trespasses and sins, made alive and set on a *new* and living way. He becomes a partaker of a *new* covenant in his blood. He is included in the promise of living in a *new* heaven and a *new* earth in which dwelleth righteousness. When a person is born again he steps into a whole new way of living because God is into making all things new. "And he that sat upon the throne said, Behold, I make all things *new*. And he said unto me, Write; for these words are true and faithful" (Rev. 21:5). Sanctifying the Lord God in our hearts will involve a lifetime of putting off the old man and putting on the *new*.

IDENTIFICATION PLEASE

When someone is asked for their identification, it generally has on it things like gender, nationality, date of birth, address, social security number and so on. It is best if this information is on some sort of a legal document like a driver's license that also has a photo ID. The more information that distinguishes your personal identity the better. Our Creator has given us a unique physical identity complete with individual fingerprints, eye-maps, and genetic code.

The Lord knows every man but He has a special spiritual identity for those who are His. 'Nevertheless, the foundation of God standeth sure, having this seal, The Lord knoweth them that are his; and, Let every one that nameth the name of Christ depart from iniquity" (2 Tim. 2:19). The identifying mark of God is His Spirit in us. He has placed His seal of ownership in our hearts. "Who hath also sealed us, and given the earnest of the Spirit in our hearts" (2 Cor. 1:22). If we do not have the Holy Spirit in our heart we are not identified as children of God. No amount of sanctified living will make up for the insurmountable lack of the absence of His Spirit. "But ye are not in the flesh but in the Spirit, if so be the Spirit of God dwell in you. Now if any man have not the Spirit of Christ, he is none of his" (Rom. 8:9). God identifies us by what He alone sees on the inside. Man can only guess what's on the inside by what he sees on the outside. Sometimes a man's judgments are right and sometimes they are wrong. "For the Lord seeth not as man seeth; for man looketh on the outward appearance, but the Lord looketh on the heart" (1 Sam. 16:7b).

SAINTS

God addresses His children with certain titles to help them know who they are in Christ. For instance, we are called saints. A saint is one who is dedicated to God and lives a holy life. There are times I don't feel like a saint, think like a saint, nor act like a saint. Have I lost my identity during these times? Well, did I earn my identity by my behavior or did I receive my identity based on the behavior of my Savior? It is Christ who presents me holy and unblamable and unreprovable in the sight of God. If my behavior does not earn my identity then my behavior cannot lose it. "And, having made peace through the blood of his cross, by him to reconcile all things unto himself—by him, I say, whether they be things in earth, or things in heaven. And you, that were once alienated and enemies in your mind by wicked works, yet now hath he reconciled in the body of his flesh through death, to present you holy and unblamable and unreprovable in his sight, if ye continue in the faith grounded and settled, and be not moved away from the hope of the gospel, which ye have heard, and which was preached to every creature that is under heaven, of which I, Paul, am made a minister" (Col. 1:20–23). When Paul addresses the church at Ephesus he calls them saints. "Paul, an apostle of Jesus Christ by the will of God, to the saints who are at Ephesus, and to the faithful in Christ Jesus" (Eph. 1:1).That is their identity in Christ and our identity in Christ. This is the faith and the good news of the gospel. Sanctification is all about bringing our behavior in line with our identity, not earning our identity by our behavior.

When one understands this truth he can't help but ask the question, "What shall we say then? Shall we continue in sin, that grace may abound? God forbid. How shall we, that are dead to sin, live any longer in it? Know ye not that, as many of us as were baptized into Jesus Christ were baptized into his death? Therefore, we are buried with him by baptism into death, that as Christ was raised up from the dead by the glory of the Father, even so we also should walk in newness of life" (Rom. 6:1–4). The new man, the spiritual man, the one raised up by the glory of the Father cannot be separated from the "should walk in newness of life". It is brought to him by the indwelling Holy Spirit. The new man comes boldly to the source of his power to help him be the person God has called him to be. "Let us therefore, come boldly unto the throne of grace, that we may obtain mercy, and find grace to help in time of need" (Heb. 4:16). Once again, grace is the divine enabling power of God for me to be all God has called me to be.

SERVANTS

Many times the apostles in their letters refer to themselves as servants of Christ. "Paul, a servant of Jesus Christ" (Rom. 1:1a). Paul who was once a persecutor of Christ now counted it an honor to serve Him. "For God is my witness, whom I serve with my spirit in the gospel of his Son, that without ceasing I make mention of you always in my prayers" (Rom. 1:9). Christ Himself took upon Himself the form of a servant and came not to be served but to serve. Christ spoke of the greatness of serving others and rebuked the disciples when they argued over who would be greatest in the kingdom of heaven. We are to serve others for Jesus' sake. "For we preach not ourselves, but Christ Jesus the

Lord, and ourselves your servants for Jesus' sake" (2 Cor. 4:5).

I heard a man say, "I don't mind being called a servant, I just don't like being treated like one." This is where most of us begin our journey with Christ. We come with our list of rights, our minimum wage, and freedom to appeal any undesirable assignment. The cry has gone up for sanctifying grace on more than one occasion when I've realized I was holding onto my own rights. By God's good grace I have made some progress, though I haven't arrived. "Not as though I had already attained, either were already perfect; but I follow after, if that I may apprehend that for which also I am apprehended of Christ Jesus. Brethren, I count not myself to have apprehended; but this one thing I do, forgetting those things which are behind, and reaching forth unto those things which are before, I press toward the mark for the prize of the high calling of God in Christ Jesus" (Phil. 3:12–14). Is it perfection God is looking for or progress? God is not asking us to "grow *into*" grace but "grow *in*" grace. If you are born again your standing is already *in* grace. "By whom also we have access by faith into this grace in which we stand, and rejoice in hope of the glory of God" (Rom. 5:2).

SOLDIERS

We are called to be soldiers in a spiritual battle with an unseen enemy regardless of our personality or temperament. The scripture tells us of the diabolical nature of our enemy, his goals along with many of his strategies. When it comes to spiritual warfare we are to be serious and alert. Satan is a skilled predator who, like a roaring lion, seeks for any unsuspecting soul he can devour. We are no match for Satan, but he is no match for Christ. The Captain of our salvation has a battle plan for victory. The Captain Himself is our strength. He has already defeated the enemy and beat him at his own game. He has provided His soldiers with weapons and armor. The scriptural call of God is to follow the Lord, resist the devil and watch him flee. "Submit yourselves, therefore, to God. Resist the devil, and he will flee from you" (Jas. 4:7).

Learning how to be a soldier begins in basic training. One of the main teachings of a military academy is learning to obey orders. Success or failure may depend on obedience to the commander. A soldier has to learn the use of arms as well as the importance of his armor and how to put it on properly; but can a soldier become a good soldier without the battle? The battle not only tries his skills but also refines them. The heat of battle and taste of victory develops confidence and character for future engagements. "Thou, therefore, endure hardness, as a good soldier of Jesus Christ. No man that warreth entangleth himself with the affairs of this life, that he may please him who hath chosen him to be a soldier" (2 Tim. 2:3–4).

It is recorded in 2 Corinthians 12:7–10 that on three occasions the Apostle Paul asked the Lord to remove the conflict he was having with the messenger of Satan. He did all the spiritual warfare he knew how to do and seemingly to no avail. In time God spoke to him and told him that His grace (sanctifying grace) was sufficient. If Paul would take glory in his infirmity the power of Christ would rest upon him. The word "power" used here is the Greek word *dynamis*, and has within its meaning the idea of "being made able or capable". "And God is able to make all grace abound toward you, that ye, always having all sufficiency in all things, may abound to every good work" (2 Cor. 9:8). By the grace of God that battle-hardened old soldier Paul, notched his belt with another victory. Physically he was growing weaker with the passing years but spiritually he was growing stronger in grace. It is no wonder Paul exhorted Timothy to be strong in grace more than any other spiritual commodity. "Thou, therefore, my son, be strong in the grace that is in Christ Jesus" (2 Tim. 2:1).

ADDITIONAL IDENTITIES

1. God has called us sons. "But, when the fullness of time was come, God sent forth his Son, made of a woman, made under the law, to redeem them that were under the law, that we might receive the adoption of sons. And because ye are sons, God hath set forth the Spirit of his Son into your hearts, crying, Abba, Father" (Gal. 4:4–6). Just think, if we're sons then we are heirs and joint heirs in the inheritance of the Father.

2. God has called us stewards. "As every man hath received the gift, even so minister the same one to another, as good stewards of the manifold grace of God" (1 Pet. 4:10). A steward manages or oversees the affairs or possessions of his master. God gives the grace, we just manage it.

3. God has called us friends. "Ye are my friends, if ye do whatever I command you. Henceforth I call you not servants; for the servant knoweth not what his Lord doeth; but I have called you friends; for all things that I have heard of my Father I have made known unto you" (John 15:14–15). Of all the identities I have in Christ, this one has taken the longest and the most grace to truly believe. As a friend I see His commandments as not burdensome for I know that he has my best interest in mind, as only a true friend can, "For this is the love of God, that we keep his commandments; and his commandments are not burdensome" (I John 5:3).

4. God calls us ambassadors in 2 Corinthians 5:20. God calls us pilgrims in 1 Peter 2:11. God calls us priests in many verses including Revelation 1:6. The identity truths of scripture are a fascinating study which helps us see ourselves as God sees us.

Christ was able to do what God wanted Him to do, largely because He knew Who He was. To be successful in our Christian walk we need to know who we are. "Let this mind be in you, which was also in Christ Jesus" (Phil. 2:5).

But He Giveth More Grace

I'd like to close this chapter with one last thought: When my faith is on trial, my flesh levels are high and my grace levels are low. I go to the throne of grace asking first for mercy on my failure, then grace to repent and make things right. I have found in every circumstance, prayer should be my first response. Prayer can give us quick access to the grace of God. Remember, things are not out of His control. In the name of Jesus, I have learned to go to God the Father in prayer and make my request known unto Him. "Be anxious for nothing, but in everything, by prayer and supplication with thanksgiving, let your requests be made known unto God. And the peace of God, which passeth all understanding, shall keep you hearts and minds through Christ Jesus" (Phil. 4:6, 7).

There are other times when I take my Bible and ask God for some truth, a truth to build me up and make me strong in grace. "And now, brethren, I commend you to God, and to the word of his grace, which is able to build you up, and to give you an inheritance among all them who are sanctified" (Acts 20:32). For the believer in Christ, the Bible is his source of truth and we do well to study it. "Study to show thyself approved unto God, a workman that needeth not to be ashamed, rightly dividing the word of truth" (2 Tim 2:15). I have found that sanctifying grace never compromises with truth. Jesus said in a prayer for his disciples, "Sanctify them through thy truth; thy word is truth" (John 17:17). Jesus, Who was full of grace and truth, also sanctified His earthly body by the truth of scripture. "And for their sakes I sanctify myself, that they also might be sanctified through the truth" (vs. 19). The Word of God is the best place to find out who you are in Christ. Knowing who you are will change how you act. Bringing your behavior in line with your identity is what sanctifying grace is all about.

CHAPTER FIVE

GRACE FOR SPEAKING

Some of the biggest problems in my life have come from one of the smallest parts of my anatomy: my tongue. Solomon said there is a time to every purpose under heaven, "a time to keep silence, and a time to speak" (Eccl. 3:7b). Most people would agree there have been times in their life when they should have been listening instead of speaking. Though often times I don't like to admit it, my tongue is revealing what's in my heart. It is more appropriate to speak when my heart is right with God. When my heart isn't right with God I would be better off to keep quiet. I have also found over the years, when my heart is right with God it's almost a natural response to be swift to hear and slow to speak. When I am out of sorts, it's just the opposite. The Scriptures give a general admonition for every Christian. "Wherefore, my beloved brethren, let every man be swift to hear, slow to speak, slow to wrath; for the wrath of man worketh not the righteousness of God" (Jas. 1:19–20). God will never endorse us speaking in anger so if there is ever a time to keep quiet; it's when we're angry. Oh, how I need grace for speaking! The tongue can be used for so many good things and bring such a blessing to the hearers, but it can also create unnecessary trouble and conflict.

Taming the Tongue

James chapter three is almost exclusively about taming the tongue. He makes statements like: if you can tame the tongue the rest of your character challenges will be a cake walk. He uses numerous illustrations: a small bit in a horse's mouth brings him under the rider's mastery and a little helm controls a great ship even under fierce winds. He compares the tongue to being like a small match able to start a fire that destroys thousands of acres of forest. If hell gets hold of the tongue, look out. It will produce a world of iniquity, full of all kinds of poison. One moment it blesses and the next moment it curses. We are told it shouldn't be this way with Christians, but that is exactly who James is writing to. It seems man has been able to tame about everything else but he can't tame his own tongue. If he is ever to tame the tongue he is going to need someone or something bigger than himself. "But He giveth more grace."

It is always profitable to hear the words of Scripture: "My brethren, be not many teachers, knowing that we shall receive the greater judgment. For in many things we all stumble. If any man offend not in word, the same is a perfect man, and able also to bridle the whole body. Behold, we put bits in the horses' mouth, that they may obey us; and we turn about their whole body. Behold also the ships, which, though they are so great and are driven by fierce winds, yet are they turned about with a very small helm, wherever the pilot willeth. Even so the tongue is a little member and boasteth great things. Behold, how great a matter a little fire kindleth! And the tongue is a fire, a world of iniquity; so is the tongue among our members that it defileth the whole body, and setteth on fire the course of nature, and is set on fire of hell. For every kind of beasts, and of birds, and of serpents, and of things in the sea, is tamed, and hath been tamed by mankind; but the tongue can no man tame; it is an unruly evil, full of deadly poison. Therewith bless we God, even the Father; and therewith curse we men, who are made after the similitude of God. Out of the same mouth proceed blessing and cursing. My brethren, these things ought not so to be" (Jas. 3:1–10).

THE RIGHT SEASONING

Have you ever said the right thing with the wrong attitude? The attitude will be what is communicated regardless of how correct or true the words are. Usually it's not *what* we say as much as *how* we say it that causes trouble. "Let your speech be always with grace, seasoned with salt, that ye may know how to answer every man" (Col. 4:6). This verse is found in the context of putting off the old man with his deeds and putting on the new man that is renewed in the image of Christ. It's in the context of husbands loving their wives and fathers loving their children. The attitude in such contexts is of the most extreme importance. No one is more discerning of how we say things than our family.

The following is not a secret but it is oftentimes over looked on how to sprinkle the seasoning of grace in our speech. "Let the word of Christ dwell in you richly, in all wisdom teaching and admonishing one another, in psalms and hymns and spiritual songs singing with grace in your hearts to the Lord. And whatever ye do in word or deed, do all in the name of the Lord Jesus, giving thanks to God and the Father by him" (Col. 3:16–17). It is out of the abundance of the heart that the mouth speaks. When there is a breakdown of grace in my speech, the problem began in my heart long before the tone of my speech revealed it. If there is anything that will tell on our heart, it's our tongue.

In Paul's letter to the church at Ephesus he is addressing similar issues concerning the walk of the new man as opposed to the old. The new man shouldn't lie but speak the truth. The new man shouldn't get angry but rather resolve conflicts before going to bed lest Satan should get a foothold during the night. If the old man has been stealing, stop. Let the new man go to work with the attitude of providing for himself as well as laying some aside for the needy. Finally, he gets to the tongue: "Let no corrupt communication proceed out of your mouth, but that which is good to the use of edifying, that it may minister grace to the hearers" (Eph. 4:29). The word "edification" means to build up or strengthen through words of love and encouragement. Oh, how I wish that every time I opened my mouth it would minister grace to my hearers. This does not mean we are to compromise with truth, but rather we are to speak the truth in love. One of the greatest evidences that we are growing in grace is when we are learning to speak the truth in love. "But, speaking the truth in love, may grow up into him in all things, who is the head, even Christ" (Eph. 4:15).

Jesus was truth personified and therefore could never compromise with falsehood, but He was not only truth in all its stark brutality, He was full of grace and truth. The right seasoning for truth is grace. "And of his fullness have all we received, and grace for grace" (John 1:16).

Jesus had the power of grace because He humbled Himself. "Let this mind be in you, which was also in Christ Jesus, who, being in the form of God, thought it not robbery to be equal with God, but made himself of no reputation, and took upon him the form of a servant, and was made in the likeness of men; And being found in fashion as a man, he humbled himself and became obedient unto death, even the death of the cross"

(Phil. 2:5–8). If there is a key, here it is: "But he giveth more grace. Wherefore he saith, God resisteth the proud, but giveth grace unto the humble" (Jas. 4:6). God can and does humble us at times but He gives us the option: "Humble yourselves in the sight of the Lord, and he shall lift you up" (vs. 10). One of the best ways I have found to humble myself is the gospel, whether preaching it to myself or preaching it to others. When a person spends time around the events of the cross of Christ, the only proper response is humility.

LOVING LIFE

I heard a preacher say, "In light of eternity, life at its worst is still worth the living." Life can be hard at times but it is still a gift from God. "In him was life; and the life was the light of men" (John 1:4). An eternal perspective on life makes all the difference in living. "And this is life eternal, that they may know thee, the only true God, and Jesus Christ, whom thou hast sent" (John 17:3). When a person is born again and begins to grow in grace and experience his new life in Christ, he gains a new love for life. "For he that will love life, and see good days, let him refrain his tongue from evil, and his lips that they speak no guile; Let him eschew evil, and do good; let him seek peace, and pursue it. For the eyes of the Lord are over the righteous, and his ears are open unto their prayers; but the face of the Lord is against them that do evil" (1 Pet. 3:10–12).

A lot of good can be done with the tongue but so can a lot of evil. Speaking words of grace that can build others up is one side of the truth. The other side of that truth is by grace learning to refrain your tongue from speaking evil, or just plain learning to keep your mouth shut. When I was growing up I heard my mother say, "If you can't say anything good, then don't say anything at all". Sometimes saying nothing is the most gracious response.

Truth in Tension

In order for any stringed instrument to make the right sound it has to be tuned to the right tension. When I over tighten truth the sound of grace leaves. When I loosen it too much, the sound of truth isn't even heard. Any truth taken to extreme soon becomes heresy.

King David was a man of many words, some gracious and some not. He knew there were times when he would be tempted to say things that would be better left unsaid. In Psalm 141, he made an urgent request for help from God: "Lord, I cry unto thee; make haste unto me; give ear unto my voice, when I cry unto thee. Let my prayer be set forth before thee as incense; and the lifting up of my hands, as the evening sacrifice. Set a watch, O Lord, before my mouth; keep the door of my lips" (Psa. 141:1–3). These words of the sweet Psalmist of Israel sound like a plea for restraining grace. Maybe his enemies had mounted an offensive against him. Maybe they were political enemies or maybe from within his own house. Maybe he felt betrayed or falsely accused. Regardless of the particulars of the situation, David knew it would be difficult to defend himself without the danger of saying to much or speaking without grace. He already knew the relationship between the words of his mouth and the condition of his heart. "Let the words of my mouth, and the meditation of my heart, be acceptable in thy sight, O Lord, my strength, and my redeemer" (Psa. 19:14).

We need to exercise a lot of restraint when it comes to defending ourselves before our accusers. At the trial of Jesus, Pilate marveled at how few words Jesus spoke in response to his accusers. "And Pilate asked him, Art thou the King of the Jews? And he, answering, said unto him, Thou sayest it. And the chief priests accused him of many things; but he answered nothing. And Pilate asked him again, saying, Answerest thou nothing? Behold how many things they witness against thee. But Jesus yet answered nothing, so that Pilate marveled" (Mk. 15:2–5). It is unnerving to false accusers when the accused appears confident his case is being tried by a higher court and a verdict of innocent will ultimately be rendered.

A Good Study

Learning how to speak with grace is no small assignment. It involves what is said as well as how it is said; the content as well as the attitude of our heart. It involves the right timing as well as the right tension. God has made it clear: man cannot tame his own tongue any more than he can tame his own heart. It requires someone stronger and wiser than the mouth and chest it lives in; it requires the God who made them both, the God of all grace. The Lord loves to teach us about ourselves by teaching us about Himself. In Thessalonians 4, Paul is speaking to the saints about the will of God for their sanctification by listing virtues that will characterize their new identity in Christ. He tells them to study, or ponder; the things that would help them live a quiet life. "And that ye study to be quiet, and to do your own business, and to work with your own hands, as we commanded you, that ye may walk honestly toward them that are outside, and that ye may have lack of nothing" (1 Thes. 4:11–12). "Quiet" may mean a literal quiet. Maybe he is suggesting there are some who shouldn't talk so much. We have one mouth and two ears, and maybe we should listen twice as much as we speak. In his second letter to these saints, he seems to address that very problem. "For we hear that there are some who walk among you disorderly, working not at all but are busybodies. Now them that are such we command and exhort, by our Lord Jesus Christ, that with quietness they work, and eat their own bread" (2 Thes. 3:11–12). As a person grows older in grace he should be able to speak less and say more. He should reduce the words and increase the content. A wise man delivers an ocean of truth in a drop of speech, rather than a drop of truth in an ocean of speech. It is sobering to think that we will give an account of every idle word that we speak. "But I say unto you that every idle word that men shall speak, they shall give account of it in the day of judgment. For by thy words thou shalt be justified, and by thy words thou shalt be condemned" (Matt. 12:36–37).

I would like to include just a few words from Solomon that might help us in our study. God gave Solomon wisdom in many things so it is only sensible to consider his proverbial wisdom with regards to grace for speaking. "In the multitude of words there lacketh not sin, but he that refraineth his lips is wise" (Prov. 10:19). There have been times I have talked myself into trouble and only talked myself in deeper trouble by trying to talk myself out. I have felt like, "Help, I'm talking and I can't shut up." "He that keepeth his mouth, keepeth his life, but he that openeth wide his lips shall have destruction" (Prov. 13:3). I have dug a pit with my mouth, only to fall in it myself. "He that hath knowledge spareth his words; and a man of understanding is of an excellent spirit. Even a fool, when he holdeth his peace, is counted wise; and he that shutteth his lips is esteemed a man of understanding" (Prov. 17:27–28). There is a saying that says, "Better to keep your mouth closed and be thought a fool than to open it and remove all doubt." As a person grows in grace it will inevitably affect his speech. As I grow older in Christ I am realizing that it takes more grace and faith to be quiet than to be quick to run my mouth.

Grace to the Hearer

The right words said in the right way at the right time can change a person's life forever. Words are powerful. Words can tear down or build up; they can help or hinder. God created all things by the power of His spoken Word and tells us: "Death and life are in the power of the tongue" (Prov. 18:21a). The Word of the gospel is powerful in any of the multitude of different languages used to communicate it. We can minister grace to the hearer by what we say as well as by what we don't say. What we don't say doesn't go unnoticed. When we don't participate in gossip it communicates volumes of grace to the hearer. Much is said when we refuse to speak evil of someone. It is a sign of weakness, not strength, when we assert our self by tearing down the character of someone else. A simple question that should be used as a rule of grace is, "Will it do the person harm, even if what I am about to say is true?" Some people never completely heal from wounds inflicted by careless words. "The words of a talebearer are as wounds, and they go down into the innermost parts" (Prov. 18:8).

Spoken words that are well-thought-out words are more likely to be words empowered with grace, good words that build up and encourage a person on in their journey of life. I am not making reference to talking religion but to saying the right words, with the right heart, at the right time. "A man hath joy by the answer of his mouth, and a word spoken in due season, how good is it!" (Prov. 15:23). I know what it is to be on the receiving end of this type of ministry. My first time to speak publicly was during a half time at a church basketball league. I nervously stumbled through and sat down. A highly educated pastor I respected came over to me, put his hand on my shoulder, looked me in the eyes and said, "Good stuff". His words connected with my soul and encouraged me more than he ever knew. I am still living off many of the kind and helpful words that have been spoken to me over the years. I truly desire to have a ministry of grace to the hearer, from a heart ruled by grace and a tongue that bears evidence of it. Thank you Lord for the promise: He giveth more grace!

CHAPTER SIX

GRACE FOR SUFFERING

Webster's dictionary defines suffering as: "to feel or bear what is painful, disagreeable or distressing, either to the body or the mind." Everyone has had to bear painful, or disagreeable or distressing things in life, some more than others. Christian or non-Christian, it is impossible to live on planet earth and not experience some measure of suffering. What is the child of God to learn about the grace of God during life's tough times? Hopefully in this chapter we will see that grace for suffering has the potential to mature us on to a closer walk with our Savior. "But the God of all grace, who hath called us unto his eternal glory by Christ Jesus, after ye have suffered awhile, make you perfect, establish, strengthen, settle you" (1 Pet. 5:10).

OUR PERFECT EXAMPLE

What better place to start our study than with the example of our Lord Jesus Christ. "For even hereunto were ye called, because Christ also suffered for us, leaving us an example, that ye should follow his steps" (1 Pet.2:21). Christ the perfect one, full of grace and truth set the standard for what it means to have grace in suffering. Having God as His Father you would think He would be exempt from any suffering. Just the opposite is true, for in the Father's plan, the Son had to suffer and refine His obedience even unto death, even the death of the cross. Jesus spoke of this to His disciples. "And he began to teach them, that the Son of man must suffer many things, and be rejected by the elders, and by the chief priests, and scribes, and be killed, and after three days rise again" (Mk. 8:31). When Jesus told them of His upcoming suffering they closed their ears to the rest of what He had to say and missed it totally. They did not want Him to suffer any more than they wanted to suffer themselves. You can't blame the disciples for their reaction, in reality who in their right mind wants to suffer, or see someone they love suffer? What the disciples did not yet understand and what they failed to hear was that the God of all grace, after Jesus had suffered awhile, would complete His redemptive plan, establish, strengthen, and settle it forever.

LEARNING OBEDIENCE

Genesis 22 records the greatest test of Abraham's and Isaac's faith. Though it had been a long journey, with numerous trials, Abraham, by the grace of God, had become a man strong in faith. For Isaac, the benefits of a godly home are about to be evidenced on the stage of God's plan of eternal redemption. Rarely is it mentioned, but it wasn't just Abraham's faith on trial, but Isaac's as well. Trials are meant to refine and purify our faith, to make us less dependent on ourselves and more dependent on the grace of God. As Abraham rose up early and together with Isaac went off to worship, I doubt there was anything he could tell himself to make his obedience easier. Questions may have crossed his mind: "Would his son plead with him for another option? Would the miracle son of promise, the son whom he loved like no other, be willing to submit his will to that of his father? Could he trust him that this was God's perfect will?" Abraham was a heartbeat away from obedience, when God stopped him and provided another sacrifice. Without this trial Abraham would never have experienced this depth of obedience. Because of their obedience God established His covenant with Abraham, Isaac, and their offspring forever.

Though Jesus was never disobedient to His Father, somehow the cross was about to move His obedience to a new level; a level that never could have been reached without the suffering of the cross. "Though he were a Son, yet learned he obedience by the things which he suffered; And being made perfect, he became the author of eternal salvation unto all them that obey him" (Heb. 5;8–9). The final hour had come. The Father was to be glorified in the Son, and the Son in the Father. "These words spoke Jesus, and lifted up his eyes to heaven, and said, Father, the hour is come; glorify thy Son, that thy Son also may glorify thee. ... I have glorified thee on the earth; I have finished the work which thou gavest me to do. And now, O Father, glorify thou me with thine own self with the glory which I had with thee before the world was" (John 17:1, 4–5). Just think; at the cross, the eternal Son of God, who was with the Father before the world began, authenticates His plan of redemption. The very word "eternal" excites faith and obedience. In light of eternity the suffering of the cross was but a moment in time, yet that moment secured eternal salvation forever to all who would come to know Christ. Just the word eternity gives greater grace to our obedience during times of suffering and affliction. "For which cause we faint not; but though our outward man perish, yet the inward man is renewed day by day. For our light affliction, which is but for a moment, worketh for us a far more exceeding and eternal weight of glory, while we look not at the things which are seen, but at the things which are not seen; for the things which are seen are temporal, but the things which are not seen are eternal" (2 Cor. 4:16–18). Eternity was a contributing factor to the enduring obedience of Jesus at the cross. "… who for the joy that was set before him endured the cross, despising the shame, and is set down at the right hand of the throne of God" (Heb. 12:2b). Jesus is not the only example we have of grace for suffering, but He is the best one.

SUFFERING FOR DOING WRONG

God's grace is greater than our sin. If this were not true no one would ever be saved. The most glorified saint in heaven was once a condemned sinner in need of God's saving grace. Scripture records the conversion of liars, thieves, murderers, harlots, pagan idol worshipers as well as the religiously lost. God is able to save them to the uttermost. "Wherefore, he is able also to save them to the uttermost that come unto God by him" (Heb. 7:25a). When a person is born again the conversion process begins. We are all set on a new course of following righteousness, but we don't all travel at the same pace. All believers must deal with their own sin, but each believer doesn't deal with the same sins to the same degree. Some people may deal with a filthy mouth but never gossip. Some people struggle with lying but not stealing. Some people struggle with laziness but would give you the shirt off their back. Some people are industrious and tireless workers but wouldn't give you a match if you were freezing to death. All of us are different, with different strengths and different vulnerabilities. I'm not sure why, whether it's the sins that shape us or us who shape the sins. Regardless, we are commanded to deal with them. "Likewise, reckon ye also yourselves to be dead unto sin, but alive unto God through Jesus Christ, our Lord. Let not sin, therefore, reign in your mortal body, that ye should obey it in its lust. Neither yield ye your members as instruments of unrighteousness unto sin, but yield yourselves unto God, as those that are alive from the dead, and your members as instruments of righteousness unto God. For sin shall not have dominion over you; for ye are not under the law but under grace" (Rom. 6:11–14).

Christians would not be told not to yield to sin unless it was possible for them to yield. Simple deduction— Christians sin! When a child of God sins he is instructed in Scripture to ask God for forgiveness. "If we confess our sins, he is faithful and just to forgive us our sins, and to cleanse us from all unrighteousness" (1 John 1:9). We should ask God for a godly sorrow over our sin. This leads us to true repentance. Confession without repentance is mockery. "Now I rejoice, not that ye were made sorry but that ye sorrowed to repentance; for ye were made sorry after a godly manner, that ye might receive damage by us in nothing. For godly sorrow worketh repentance to salvation not to be repented of; but the sorrow of the world worketh death" (2 Cor. 7:9–10). Repentance is not something we can manufacture on our efforts alone, as in all spiritual things it requires the grace of God. "Or despiseth thou the riches of his goodness and forebearance and long-suffering, not knowing that the goodness of God leadeth thee to repentance?" (Rom. 2:4)

Sin that is confessed and forsaken and is properly dealt with through the grace of Christ may still have consequences. "But let none of you suffer as a murderer, or as a thief, or as an evildoer, or as a busybody in other men's matters" (1 Pet. 4:15). If you murder, deal with your sin in the Biblical way as earlier described but expect to go to jail. If you steal something, make restitution. It may take you four times as long to pay it back but do it. By gossiping you injure the character of a person. In humility and grace determine to rid yourself of this sin while accepting the consequences of broken relationships as part of your Christian training. Peter says it best that when you do wrong, take your lumps. "For what glory is it if, when ye are buffeted for your faults, ye shall take it patiently?" (1 Pet. 2:20). God extends grace to us even when we are suffering the result of our sin. David knew God and knew what it was to sin against Him. He knew what it was to reap the sorrow and regret of sin. He also knew the gracious nature of God. "Bless the Lord, O my soul, and all that is within me, bless his holy name. Bless the Lord, O my soul, and forget not all his benefits, Who forgiveth all thine iniquities, who healeth all thy diseases, Who redeemeth thy life from destruction, who crowneth thee with loving kindness and tender mercies, Who satisfieth thy mouth with good things, so that thy youth is renewed like the eagle's. The Lord executeth righteousness and judgment for all who are oppressed. He made known his ways unto Moses, his acts unto the children of Israel. The Lord is merciful and gracious, slow to anger, and plenteous in mercy. He will not always chide; neither will he keep his anger forever. He hath not dealt with us after our sins, nor rewarded us according to our iniquities. For as the heavens are high above the earth, so great is his mercy toward them that fear him. As far as the east is from the west, so far hath he removed our transgressions from us. As a father pitieth his children, so the Lord pitieth them that fear him. For he knoweth our frame; he remembereth that we are dust" (Psa. 103:1–14). Suffering for the wrong we do is part of God's chastisement which eventually produces righteousness in our lives. "Now no chastening for the present seemeth to be joyous, but grievous; nevertheless, afterward it yieldeth the peaceable fruit of righteousness unto them who are exercised by it" (Heb. 12:11). Take your lumps and know that He giveth more grace.

SUFFERING FOR DOING RIGHT

In my opinion, suffering for doing wrong is easier than suffering for doing right because if we are honest, we expect to suffer for doing wrong. Yet Scripture clearly tells us to expect suffering for doing right as well. "But and if ye suffer for righteousness' sake, happy are ye; and be not afraid of their terror, neither be troubled" (1 Pet.3:14). If a person is going to do what is right in the eyes of the Lord and walk in the ways of godliness, he can expect some measure of persecution. "Yea, and all that will live godly in Christ Jesus shall suffer persecution" (2 Tim. 3:12). As we grow in grace we grow less like the world. We relate to less of its philosophies, enjoy less of its pleasures and find ourselves becoming pilgrims and strangers in a foreign land. We lose our taste for things that are not after Christ. "Beware lest any man spoil you through philosophy and vain deceit, after the tradition of men, after the rudiments of the world, and not after Christ" (Col. 2:8). The Christian is to live uprightly in the midst of a sinful world, loving people and all the while learning to hate the sin that is destroying them. "That ye may be blameless and harmless, children of God, without rebuke, in the midst of a crooked and perverse nation, among whom ye shine as lights in the world" (Phil. 2:15). The memory of our pre-Christ condition moves our hearts to see the lost become saved. If our minds and actions have at all been transformed by the grace of God we should be willing to risk a little ridicule for the sake of others, especially if we have ever mocked a Christian who shared the gospel with us. "For the time past of our life may suffice us to have wrought the will of the Gentiles, when we walked in lasciviousness, lusts, excess of wine, revellings, carousings, and abominable idolatries, in which they think it strange that ye run not with them to the same profligacy, speaking evil of you" (1 Pet. 4:3–4).

The world hated Christ because His good life was a living testimony which in itself brought conviction to the sinful ways of man. Jesus told His disciples they could expect the same if they were to follow Him. "If the world hate you, ye know that it hated me before it hated you. If ye were of the world, the world would love its own; but because ye are not of the world, but I have chosen you out of the world, therefore the world hateth you. Remember the word that I said unto you. The servant is not greater than his Lord. If they have persecuted me, they will also persecute you; if they have kept my saying, they will keep yours also" (John 15:18–20). Being warned by the Lord in advance we should not be taken by surprise. We should be prepared with the proper response of grace. "Bless them who persecute you; bless, and curse not" (Rom. 12:14). I have seen the power of a spoken blessing break the power of a curse. I have kept myself from being over taken with evil by overcoming evil with good. I have wished people well who have wished me evil and the shock of it disarms them almost immediately. In some cases they turn from persecutor to supporter within minutes. I have seen a kind humble response to a malicious hateful word diffuse a potentially explosive situation. I have also seen a retaliatory word spoken in pride take a bad situation and made it much worse. "A soft answer turneth away wrath, but grievous words stir up anger" (Prov. 15:1). Christ is always our best example, especially when it comes to suffering for doing right. "For even hereunto were ye called, because Christ also suffered for us, leaving us and example, that ye should follow his steps; Who did no sin, neither was guile found in his mouth; Who, when he was reviled, reviled not again; when he suffered, he threatened not, but committed himself to him that judgeth righteously" (1 Pet. 2:21–23).

CHRISTIAN PERSECUTION

The early church was born in Jerusalem and was made up primarily of Jews. When these early believers came to trust Jesus as their Messiah they knew it would cost them. Doubtless part of that cost was persecution. They were expelled from the synagogue, which was the very center of Jewish life. Families disowned them. Many lost their jobs, were beaten, arrested on false charges and some were even executed. As the church spread throughout the world, persecution spread with it. There was fierce persecution, not only in Rome itself, but throughout many parts of the Roman Empire.

Followers of the Christian faith have always faced persecution. Today the number one persecuted religion in the world is Christianity. Christians are being arrested, tortured, and even killed in many parts of the world. Having grown up in the United States, I have known only religious freedom and nothing of religious persecution. It seems America is joining the world in becoming increasingly hostile towards Christ. Genuine persecution may be on the way and arrive quicker than we think. In my personal preparation I have determined to strengthen three areas of my faith. I have chosen to (1)wake up with regard to the increasing hostility toward Christians and Jews worldwide, (2) to walk more circumspectly in my private devotions to God and public witness for God, and (3)to redeem the time with more of an eternal perspective on who I want to please in this brief temporal life. "Wherefore, he saith, Awake thou that sleepest, and arise from the dead, and Christ shall give thee light. See, then, that ye walk circumspectly, not as fools but as wise, Redeeming the time, because the days are evil" (Eph. 5:14–16). I have chosen to strengthen my love for Jerusalem, Israel and the Jews, and to stand in support of them as God's chosen people. If a Christian doesn't love the Jews, he doesn't love Jesus, for He was a Jew. If you don't love Israel, you don't love the Word of God for it was handed down to us by Israelite prophets and scribes. If you don't love Jerusalem, you won't love your new home.; "And I, John, saw the holy city, New Jerusalem, coming down from God out of heaven, prepared as a bride adorned for her husband" (Rev. 21:2). I have chosen to be bolder in proclaiming the gospel and seek to be more courageous in living it. Persecution is as old as Cain and Abel; it's nothing new. But it's new for me. I have little to no spiritual framework for living within persecution. I find myself an aging Tom Harmon, living in a rapidly becoming anti-Christian world. In these changing times more grace will be needed and more grace is exactly what He gives.

A Special Blessing

God promises a special blessing to those who, through the grace of God, learn how to look at suffering as part and parcel of following Christ. "Blessed are they who are persecuted for righteousness' sake; for theirs is the kingdom of heaven. Blessed are ye when men shall revile you, and persecute you, and shall say all manner of evil against you falsely, for my sake. Rejoice, and be exceedingly glad; for great is your reward in heaven;

for so persecuted they the prophets who were before you" (Mt. 5:10–12).

The choice inherent within persecution boils down to the question of whether a man is going to live a life pleasing to God or man. The Apostle Paul asked himself the question: "Do I seek to please men or God?" He answered himself in the same verse: if I seek to please men I should not be the servant of Christ (see Gal. 1:10). I believe Paul had come to the place in his life where he made the decision that if he pleased Christ it didn't matter whom he offended, and if he offended Christ it didn't matter whom he pleased. It's obvious not everyone is going to be pleased when we become servants of Christ. We should expect some opposition and face it with the grace of Christ.

A somewhat comforting truth is this: persecution isn't really against us but against Christ. When Jesus spoke to Paul on his way to Damascus he made it clear: "Saul, Saul, why persecutes thou me? And he said, Who art thou, Lord? And the Lord said, I am Jesus, whom thou persecutest" (Acts 9:4b–5a). Won't it be a blessed honor to join the sacred throng of those who rejoice in that they were counted worthy to suffer for Christ's sake?

SUFFERING AS PART OF GOD'S SOVEREIGN DESIGN

My life's verse is Philippians 3:10: "That I may know him, and the power of his resurrection, and the fellowship of his sufferings, being made conformable unto his death." The power of His resurrection could never have occurred without His death. His death was inseparably related to His suffering. Suffering was just plain part of God's sovereign plan of redemption. Hudson Taylor, a missionary to China, said, "God never wastes suffering." God has a plan for everything and sometimes it includes suffering. Taylor is regarded as a man who lived in the power of the resurrection and had a great impact on China as well as foreign missions throughout the world. He, like Jesus, was a man of sorrows and acquainted with grief and suffering. He endured unbelievable hardships throughout his ministry. He endured the trials in his life because he saw them as part of God's plan to strengthen his faith and deepen his walk. Our theology can be flawless with regard to the sovereign will of God and suffering, but until it is tested, it's only what we say we believe. Attempting to write on this causes me to realize how little I actually know of the subject. I'm not sure this truth can move from our head to our heart without the experience. Things are learned during suffering that can't be learned in any other school. I know in my head that suffering and death are prerequisites for living in resurrection power, but without the experience, I'm not sure I know it in my heart. I want the benefits of the latter end of Job without graduating from his school to get them.

JOB

Job is the classic illustration of suffering according to the sovereign will of God. Job is where God wants him to be, doing what God wants him to do and, as far as we know, going where God wants him to go. Nobody knows our theology better than God and God knew Job had good theology. Job's theology was sound: he was a man who reverenced God and shunned evil. He was a praying man and made sacrifices to God on behalf of his family. He gave to the poor and stood up for the oppressed. He knew to accept adversity at the hand of God as well as good. His theology was sound, and then, it was tested.

From a perfect calm his life became a whirlwind of suffering. Out of that whirlwind God revealed Himself and the power of the resurrected life. In one day all of his children die and he loses all his financial wealth. Job's response is a testimony to the grace of God. This is the response of Job upon the arrival of this horrible news. "Then Job arose, and tore his mantle, and shaved his head, and fell down upon the ground, and worshiped. And said, Naked came I out of my mother's womb, and naked shall I return there. The Lord gave, and the Lord hath taken away; blessed be the name of the Lord. In all this Job sinned not, nor charged God with folly" (Job 1:20–22).

Next, he came down with an epidemic of painful boils from head to toe. His wife sunk into despair, lost faith, and suggested suicide. On the heels of this, three close friends try to put the blame on some secret sin Job must have been harboring in his life. Men can be miserable comforters who add affliction rather than relieve it.

Job was probably at his lowest when God spoke to him out of the whirlwind. Job was quickly humbled in the presence of his mighty God. The eternal God of all grace never required him to understand his momentary troubles, just to trust Him. There is no command in scripture, "Thou shalt understand God." No, instead we are told over and over to trust Him. "Trust in the Lord with all thine heart, and lean not unto thine own understanding. In all thy ways acknowledge him, and he shall direct thy paths". (Prov. 3:5–6). This kind of truth is much easier to preach than it is to live. It is definitely impossible to live without the sustaining grace of Almighty God.

Job was well grounded in his theology and could even hear himself preaching it, but without the experience he would have remained blind to the power of it. "I have heard of thee by the hearing of the ear, but now mine eye seeth thee" (Job 42:5). He saw things in his life that he never would have seen. Things he needed to repent of, things he didn't even know were there. Oh, how cleansing for Job to see these things and come to a new depth of knowing and loving God, the Giver and Sustainer of his soul. At the time of Job, God considered him to be the best man in all the earth. In his final words, you see the best get even better. "Wherefore I abhor myself, and repent in dust and ashes" (Job 42:6).

Job lived to see God double everything for him, but worldly abundance stands in the shadows of the things he learned of God. It was the things he learned that would be what made his latter end better than his first. The book of Job is recommended to all who may be going through suffering. It is rich in giving a proper balance to the grace of God amidst the suffering of life.

CHAPTER SEVEN

GRACE FOR SINGING

Beginning with the Old Testament saints to the present church age, the Bible records that God's people sang. The Israelites sang after they were delivered from land of captivity. "Then sang Moses and the children of Israel this song unto the Lord, and spoke, saying, I will sing unto the Lord, for he hath triumphed gloriously; the horse and his rider hath he thrown into the sea. The Lord is my strength and song, and he is become my salvation; he is my God, and I will prepare him an habitation; my father's God, and I will exalt him" (Ex. 15:1–2).

This song of Moses will be sung in heaven at the final deliverance of the saints. "And they sing the song of Moses, the servant of God, and the song of the Lamb, saying, Great and marvelous are thy works, Lord God Almighty; just and true are thy ways, thou King of saints. Who shall not fear thee, O Lord, and glorify thy name? For thou only art holy; for all nations shall come and worship before thee; for thy judgments are made manifest" (Rev. 15:3–4).

Throughout the Old Testament we see the importance of song. David sang and wrote music. He also played instruments and led singing during corporate worship. Asaph was a song leader and played the cymbals when the Levites (carried?) the Ark. He is also credited with writing twelve psalms and establishing a school of music. Solomon employed a 2000 member choir that sang during every Sabbath worship. The morning and evening sacrifice began and ended with music and song.

People of Biblical faith still sing and write spiritual songs, perhaps more than any other religion in the world. True worshipers can't help but sing to the Lord. Even if we can't carry a tune, play an instrument, or even tap our foot to a beat, the God of all grace puts a song in our heart. "Make a joyful noise unto the Lord, all ye lands, Serve the Lord with gladness; come before his presence with singing" (Psa. 100:1–2).

MY HOBBY

A number of years ago I began collecting Christian hymnals and song books. I made mention of it several times from the pulpit and friends began to pick them up for me at yard sales and so on. The oldest one I have was copyrighted in 1835. I soon had more boxes of song books than I had room for so I reduced them to a select group of 200. I love to read through them and occasionally sing a familiar one. My wife, Joyce, and I love to sing together. We carry a hymnal in our car and sometimes during our trips we open it up and sing to the Lord. Christian songs are written on a variety of topics but they all are directed toward God. There are songs that celebrate certain holy days like Christmas and Easter. There are songs of testimony, trials, and thanksgiving. There are worship songs, wedding songs, evangelistic songs, and the list goes on. Regardless of the circumstances, Christians seem to put things to music and song, more than any other religious group in the world. My favorite kind of songs are the ones that focus on God's wonderful work of salvation. To me the theme of the Bible is the glory of God in the redemption of man. When the song has a clear message of my Savior and redemption, it's easy for me to enter into worship and praise. "Let the word of Christ dwell in you richly, in all wisdom teaching and admonishing one another, in psalms and hymns and spiritual songs singing with grace in your hearts to the Lord" (Col. 3:16).

A Good Habit

Part of sanctifying grace is establishing good habits. Scripture records some of the good habits of godly people. Job prayed for his family every morning, as was his custom. Ezra would study the Scriptures daily as was his custom. Daniel and David prayed three times a day as a matter of habit. Jesus went to the synagogue every Sabbath as was His custom, and so on. I have found it a good habit to daily think on the gospel of my salvation. Many times pondering my salvation has produced strength for my faith and joy in my heart; joy that produces a song of praise in my heart.

Salvation, joy, and singing seem to go together. "Behold, God is my salvation; I will trust, and not be afraid; for the Lord, even the Lord, is my strength and my song; he also is become my salvation. Therefore, with joy shall ye draw water out of the wells of salvation" (Isa. 12:2–3). Nothing can take our salvation from us; therefore, no situation, no matter how difficult, should be able to take away our joy. Salvation and joy are inseparably linked together. I have purposed not to let anything steal my joy. Sin can't steal my salvation, so I refuse to let it steal my joy. "Restore unto me the joy of thy salvation, and uphold me with a willing spirit" (Psa. 51:12). David knew he hadn't lost his salvation; he just lost the joy of his salvation.

Habakkuk was a prophet during some of Israel's darkest days. The nation of Israel as a whole had wandered from the ways of God. The blessing of godliness was gone and the people were struggling politically, economically and, worst of all spiritually. For few things are as dry to the soul as religious activity without heart. The old prophet was not happy, but he hadn't lost his song of joy. "Although the fig tree shall not blossom, neither shall fruit be in the vines; the labor of the olive shall fail, and the fields shall yield no food; the flock shall be cut off from the fold, and there shall be no herd in the stalls; Yet I will rejoice in the Lord, I will joy in the God of my salvation. The Lord God is my strength, and he will make my feet like hinds feet, and he will make me walk upon mine high places. To the chief singer on my stringed instruments" (Hab. 3:17–19). This is the grace we have access to and in which we can assuredly stand—grace for singing.

The Holy Spirit had instructed Paul to leave Troas and go to Macedonia and preach. Philippi was the first church to be established there. There was great success in the ministry as well as great opposition. "For a great door, and effectual, is opened unto me, and there are many adversaries" (1 Cor. 16:9). Paul and Silas were arrested without any formal charge, beaten for an unknown crime and thrown into prison. Their backs were sore and very possibly caked with dried blood from the beating. More than likely they were treated disrespectfully by the arresting soldiers. The prison they were remanded to was not like the prisons of today. It was cold, damp and smelled like a pit toilet. Ventilation and comfort wasn't high on the priority list for the prisons of that day. The guards were bound to keep them, not necessarily care for them. Hunger and thirst may have added to their affliction. Some of his fellow inmates may have been dangerous and violent men.

These were hard times yet Paul was determined to finish his course with joy. Knowing in Whom he had believed, and that He was able to keep that which he had committed unto Him against that final day, he began to rejoice and praise the God of his salvation. "And at midnight Paul and Silas prayed, and sang praises unto God; and the prisoners heard them" (Acts 16:25). God also heard them and immediately went to work on their behalf. "And suddenly there was a great earthquake, so that the foundations of the prison were shaken; and immediately all the doors were opened, and every one's bands were loosed" (vs. 26). They began singing at midnight and joy came in the morning.

The jailer panicked seeing all the doors open and the men free of their bonds. His head would roll and he knew it. A suicidal thought crossed his mind and with sword in hand he was about to act upon it when; "Paul cried with a loud voice, saying, Do thyself no harm; for we are all here" (vs. 28). Within moments the jailer is asking Paul and Silas, "Sirs, what must I do to be saved?" The grace they had for singing, led to grace for a man's salvation.

Paul and Silas were revealing the presence of the Holy Spirit in them. They weren't singing for the jailer or the inmates. They were singing to the Lord. They were praising God for His goodness and giving Him thanks in the midst of their misery and affliction. They were under the influence of grace. "And be not drunk with wine, in which is excess, but be filled with the Spirit. Speaking to yourselves in psalms and hymns and spiritual songs, singing and making melody in your heart to the Lord, Giving thanks always for all things unto God and the Father in the name of our Lord Jesus Christ" (Eph. 5:18–20). There is always grace for a song about salvation. Here's a little chorus I wrote a number of years ago. I still sing it to the Lord from time to time and it brings joy to my soul:

"The Son's up and it's hard to be down,
the Son's up, giving light all around,
the Son's up, how can anybody frown,
the Son is up and it's hard to be down.

The Son died on a cross one day,
and his blood washed all my sins away,
but best of all he rose up from the grave,
the Son is up and it's hard to be down.

The Son's up and he's coming back for me,
the Son's up, with him forever I will be,
the Son's for all eternity,
the Son is up and it's hard to be down."

GRACE FOR SERVING

What a privilege to be a servant to the God of all grace. Can you imagine a boss who never tells you to do something he wouldn't do and hasn't already done himself? A boss who treats you like a son rather than just a hired hand? A boss who is in business for your success, not his? A boss who came up through the ranks and knows the challenges of submission to authority? A boss who gives you an assignment then works alongside you till the job is done? A boss who always pays you more than you deserve, then gives you a surprise bonus at the end? It's no wonder the title "servant of God" was a favorite among the apostles. "Paul, a servant of Jesus Christ" (Rom. 1:1a); "James, a servant of God and of the Lord Jesus Christ" (Jas. 1:1a); "Simon Peter, a servant and an apostle of Jesus Christ" (2 Pet. 1:1a); "Jude, the servant of Jesus Christ, and brother of James" (Jude 1:1a). Some of the greatest grace in serving comes in knowing what an honor it is to serve the true and living God.

SERVING PEOPLE

Let's cut to the chase: no man can serve God without serving others. Jesus was constantly serving people. He answered their questions, healed their diseases, calmed their storms and even provided them with food. He made it especially clear to His disciples that He was among them as one who served. He taught them a special point about service when he filled a basin of water and washed their feet. This unnerved them and brought about a violent reaction from Peter, "Thou shalt never wash my feet." Jesus made it clear that no one with unwashed feet had any relationship with Him. When Peter understood the imagery he swung too far the other way and wanted Jesus to give him a complete bath. Jesus said he was already bathed clean; it was only his feet which were dirty from the journey. Here was the lesson He wanted them to learn. "So after he had washed their feet, and had taken his garments, and was seated again, he said unto them, Know ye what I have done to you? Ye call me Master and Lord; and ye say well; for so I am. If I, then, your Lord and Master, have washed your feet, ye also ought to wash one another's feet. For I have given you an example, that ye should do as I have done to you. Verily, verily, I say unto you, The servant is not greater than his lord; neither he that is sent greater than he that sent him. If ye know these things, happy are ye if ye do them" (John 13:12–17).

Here the crowning jewel of the character of Christ really shines. In fact it's the only character quality He ever claimed of Himself. "Come unto me, all ye that labor and are heavy laden, and I will give you rest. Take my yoke upon you, and learn of me; for I am meek and lowly in heart, and ye shall find rest unto your souls" (Mt. 11:28–29).

Meekness is not weakness; it's just the opposite. It's direct access to the strength of God's grace. Jesus served others out of the strength of humility. He couldn't have ministered without humility. It takes grace to serve others. Humility accesses grace which is the divine enabling power of God for me to do all He has called me to do.

We are called to serve others. "For we preach not ourselves, but Christ Jesus the Lord, and ourselves your servants for Jesus' sake" (2 Cor.4:5). You can preach yourself and serve yourself without grace, but if a man is going to preach Christ and serve others he's going to need grace. The greatest friend to serving grace is humility. "But he giveth more grace. Wherefore he saith, God resisteth the proud, but giveth grace unto the humble" (Jas. 4:6). Humbling yourself means having a submissive will to another. "In like manner, ye younger, submit yourselves unto the elder. Yea, all of you be subject one to another, and be clothed with humility; for God resisteth the proud, and giveth grace to the humble. Humble yourselves, therefore, under the mighty hand of God, that he may exalt you in due time" (1 Pet. 5:5–6). The will of God is for us to serve others. Humble submission to His will does not eliminate conflicts in serving but it does access the grace of God that resolves those conflicts. The key to conflict resolution is humility which is acknowledging my absolute dependence on God. Learning to live within humility is the great process called growing in grace.

A Good Service Record

My father worked 31 years as a factory worker in the auto industry. He told me numerous times the best reference in your service record is dependability. Were you faithful to be there every day you were expected to be there? Did you show up for work or were there a lot of absences on your record? Regardless of your skills or other job qualifications, if you don't show up for work you can't give productive labor. Labor is work. Work is necessary to get the job done.

The work of God to redeem man was no small job and work was required in order to complete it. "But Jesus answered them, My Father worketh hitherto, and I work" (John 5:17). Jesus also said: "I must work the works of him that sent me, while it is day; the night cometh, when no man can work" (John 9:4). Near the end of His ministry Jesus could say with confidence, "I have glorified thee on the earth; I have finished the work which thou gavest me to do" (John 17:4).

JUST A FIELD HAND

When I sensed the call of God to the preaching ministry I remember telling Him I had no real skills or qualifications for the job. I was just a laborer. As time went on I discovered God was just looking for laborers.; "Therefore said he unto them, The harvest truly is great, but the laborers are few; pray ye, therefore the Lord of the harvest, that he would send forth laborers into his harvest" (Lu.10:2).

My entire life I have wanted to be a farmer. Maybe it started early in life due to spending summers with my Grandpa on his dairy farm or maybe it was just in me. Even now farming has a special place in my heart. Farm labor is hard work, but it's the kind of work I felt I could do. If we have any special talents or skills, they are gifts from God; yet all the talents in the world are worthless without the labor to go along with them. Over the years I've come to realize that labor is all any of us have to offer Him. By the grace of God you take what you have and do what you can. It's God who builds His kingdom. "Who, then, is Paul, and who is Apollos, but ministers by whom ye believed, even as the Lord gave to every man? I have planted, Apollos watered, but God gave the increase. So, then, neither is he that planteth anything, neither he that watereth, but God that giveth the increase. Now he that planteth and he that watereth are one; and every man shall receive his own reward according to his own labor. For we are laborers together with God; ye are God's cultivated field, ye are God's building. According to the grace of God which is given unto me" (1 Cor. 3:5–10a).

More often than not, just prior to signing my name, I write, "Just a field hand." It reminds me of the privilege that is mine and gives me perspective about who and what I am. I am by the grace of God a field hand. Paul said it this way: "For I am the least of the apostles, that am not fit to be called an apostle, because I persecuted the church of God. But by the grace of God I am what I am; and his grace, which was bestowed upon me, was not in vain, but I labored more abundantly than they all; yet not I, but the grace of God which was with me" (1 Cor. 15:9–10). Paul also begins and ends all of his letters with "Grace to you". Servants of God are servants of grace, by grace.

GRACE FOR STEWARDSHIP

A fitting way to conclude this book is with a look at the truth of our identity as stewards. God refers to His children as stewards. A steward is a person who carefully oversees the possessions or affairs of another. Our life is a gift from God entrusted to us to oversee and manage for His glory. Salvation is also a gift of His grace. "For by grace are ye saved through faith; and that not of yourselves, it is the gift of God—not of works, lest any man should boast" (Eph. 2:8–9). I want to be a good steward of this grace and never treat my salvation with shame or contempt. My goal is rather to manage it with reverence and deep affection.

God gives His children spiritual gifts to oversee as well. "Having then gifts differing according to the grace that is given to us, whether prophecy, let us prophesy according to the proportion of faith; Or ministry, let us wait on our ministering; or he that teacheth, on teaching; Or he that exhorteth, on exhortation; he that giveth, let him do it with liberality; he that ruleth, with diligence; he that showeth mercy, with cheerfulness" (Rom. 12:6–8).

God's spiritual gift to me is preaching. Being a good manager of this gift requires serious study of the Bible. I must preach the truth of the Word with clarity and passion. I must know how to stir up the gift of God that is in me and be content with it for my life's work. Preaching is my foundational gift and I must not stray too far from it; other ministries are for other ministers. I have seen men lose their ministry by moving away from their gifts and callings.

When a man desires to be in church leadership there are certain qualifications that are to be met. He is to consider himself as the steward of God. "For a bishop must be blameless, as the steward of God, not self-willed, not soon angry, not given to wine, not violent, not given to filthy lucre, but a lover of hospitality, a lover of good men, sober-minded, just, holy, temperate, holding fast the faith word as he hath been taught, that he may be able by sound doctrine both to exhort and to confute the opposers" (Titus 1:7–9). An elder, as the steward of God's Church, is to model true Christian behavior before the people he is serving. Elders do not own the church; they are however, to oversee it and to be stewards of it. They have been given the responsibility of guiding and protecting it with all diligence. The apostle Paul emphasizes this in his farewell to the Ephesian elders: "Take heed, therefore, unto yourselves, and to all the flock, over which the Holy Spirit hath made you overseers, to feed the church of God, which he hath purchased with his own blood. For I know this, that after my departing shall grievous wolves enter in among you, not sparing the flock. Also of your own selves shall men arise, speaking perverse things, to draw away disciples after them. Therefore, watch, and remember, that for the space of three years I ceased not to warn everyone night and day with tears" (Acts 20:28–31). We are called to be stewards of our salvation, stewards of our spiritual gifts, and if in leadership, stewards of the Church of God.

What Makes a Good Steward?

Scripture often refers to the Christian life in athletic terms. Sports like boxing, wrestling, and marathon running are mentioned. As in any sport winning the prize is an important goal. When an athletic scout is looking for an athlete for a particular sport, he has certain qualities in mind. The qualities of a good basketball player are quite simple: can he jump, shoot, dribble, and pass the ball? It also helps if he is tall. Qualities of good football players are strength, speed, durability, and good peripheral vision. Qualities of a good bull rider are courage, balance, and just plain toughness. As there are preferred qualities for every kind of sport athlete so there are for stewards. So what makes a person a good steward of the grace of God? "As every man hath received the gift, even so minister the same one to another, as good stewards of the manifold grace of God" (1 Pet. 4:10).

Before we consider some preferred qualities of a good steward, let's look at manifold grace. Why grace is called the manifold grace of God? The word manifold means many and varied. I think God's grace is many and varied because there are so many different people with so many different needs. Christ finds people in varied circumstances and situations; some are open to the gospel and some are closed. Some are not far from the kingdom and others couldn't be farther. Nothing but the grace of God has the flexibility and power to meet the many and varied conditions of man. Besides the readily apparent differences there are also many mysteries in the performance of God's grace in the lives of men. Can you imagine the many different needs that must be met in grace to understand the gospel of salvation? After salvation there is grace for sanctification, service, leadership, repentance, and grace for the multitude of spiritual gifts. Therefore it requires a good steward to be an effective minister of this manifold grace.

All those who have received the gift of grace have been commissioned to be a good steward of it. A good steward of grace may have many good characteristics as he ministers grace to others but one seems to stand above all the others. This quality is often unnoticed among men but held in high esteem by God. Paul makes mention of it in his first letter to the church at Corinth. "Let a man so account of us, as of the ministers of Christ, and stewards of the mysteries of God. Moreover, it is required in stewards, that a man be found faithful" (1 Cor. 4:1–2).

I am so glad stewards do not have to be brilliant, just faithful. They don't have to be fruitful, just faithful. They don't have to be wealthy, or handsome, or successful, or talented, or strong, or healthy, or influential, or clever, or popular, or even well liked, just faithful. It is a worthy goal in life just to live

103

in hopes of hearing the Lord say, "Well done, thou good and faithful servant" (Mt. 25:21b).

Paul encouraged Timothy to hold the truths he had learned about grace and commit them to faithful men who would be able to teach others also. Faithful men are hard to find. "Most men will proclaim every one his own goodness; but a faithful man, who can find" (Prov. 20:6). I have found a number of faithful men scattered throughout the Scripture and at least two things seem to characterize all of them. We will take a look at the example of Abraham.

A Faithful Man

Obedience isn't always easy but it's one of the marks of a faithful man. Abraham, the father of faith, found the imputed righteousness of God through grace. This same grace led him to obey God and leave his native home in Chaldea. He left the known for the unknown banking only on a promise from God. He lived as a foreigner in a foreign land with Isaac and Jacob, heirs with him of the same promise. He looked for a city he never saw except through the eyes of faith. Yet he died in faith because he lived in faith. "These all died in faith, not having received the promises but having seen them afar off, and were persuaded of them, and embraced them, and confessed that they were strangers and pilgrims on the earth" (Heb. 11:13). His obedience to God won him the title, Faithful Abraham. "And the scripture, foreseeing that God would justify the Gentiles through faith, preached before the gospel unto Abraham, saying, In thee shall all nations be blessed. So, then, they who are of faith are blessed with faithful Abraham" (Gal. 3:8–9). This caliber of obedience is an obedience that only shines forth from a reverent heart, one sobered at the mighty grace of God that has been extended to it. The grace of God was the foundation of Abraham's faith and he nurtured it throughout his life. He knew the truth, "He giveth more grace." When a man loses his reverence for God, his grace levels will drop and he will obey only when it's convenient.

Humility is open and unashamed dependence on God. It is impossible to offend a humble person. God will humble us but He gives us the option. "Humble yourselves in the sight of the Lord, and he shall lift you up" (Jas. 4:10). Humility, louder than any other voice is saying to God, "I trust you!" I love the old hymn:

'Tis so sweet to trust in Jesus,
Just to take Him at His word;
Just to rest upon His promise;
Just to know, thus saith the Lord.

Jesus, Jesus, how I trust Him!
How I've proved Him o'er and o'er!
Jesus, Jesus, Precious Jesus!
O for grace to trust Him more!
    Louisa M.R. Stead

What a wonderful way to glorify God: "That we should be to the praise of his glory, who first trusted in Christ" (Eph. 1:12). Just a thought—any theology that doesn't lead to doxology, probably is not Biblical theology.

Moving right along—God takes notice of both pride and humility. "God resisteth the proud, and giveth grace to the humble. Humble yourselves, therefore, under the mighty hand of God, that he may exalt you in due time" (1 Pet. 5:5c–6).

God saw the humility in Abraham and lifted him up. One of the most notable accounts of his humility occurred between him and his nephew Lot. "And there was a strife between the herdsmen of Abram's cattle and the herdsmen of Lot's cattle; and the Canaanite and the Perizzite dwelt then in the land. And Abram said unto Lot, Let there be no strife, I pray thee, between me and thee, and between my herdsmen and thy herdsmen; for we are brethren. Is not the whole land before thee? Separate thyself, I pray thee, from me: if thou will take the left hand, then I will go to the right; or if thou depart to the right hand, then I will go to the left" (Gen. 13:7–9).

Abraham had to bring a resolution to the obvious conflict between Lot and himself. There needed to be a strong show of grace. More than likely the herdsmen from both camps had listened to them talk about the gospel, now they needed to see it. It is very possible they had spoken of the grace of God to the Canaanites and Perizzites and they were in need of seeing just how this grace worked. Abraham felt the burden and humbled himself. There was precious little humility in Lot for if there had been, he would not have made this appeal to his Uncle Abram. You see, in one direction was the well-watered plain with its lush grazing land as well as towns that would be good for commerce. In the other direction was the Judean wilderness, where only a few nomadic goat herders competed for what little water and grazing there was. Lot chose all the best for himself and gave the leftovers to Abram. But the God who giveth more grace gave Abram great grace and he responded in humility.

When Lot was taken captive by an invading group of kings, Abraham didn't hesitate a moment but left his own flocks unguarded and with his men delivered Lot. He, his family, and his belongings were all returned safely.

Lot's proud life continued to spiral downward until God had him forcibly removed from Sodom. He had told his wife about God but she didn't believe his words, she believed his life. She looked back to the things she and her husband both had come to value, and in doing so, she was turned into a pillar of salt.

Lot eventually died in a cave after two incestuous relations with his daughters. Abraham on the other hand became strong in faith and lived a life that brought glory to God. In the end he died in faith the father of many nations even as God had promised. His life was a great adventure from beginning to end. His legacy lives on to this day. Oh the promises that have been fulfilled because of his humility and obedient faith, truly he was a good steward of the manifold grace of God.

In Closing

Writing a book on grace has been good for me. There is plenty I need to learn, and because of grace I am hopeful I will. His grace is sufficient for me and in moments when I think it's not, He giveth more grace. Sometimes He giveth more grace when I think I have enough. Oh, praise Him for His divine enabling power. Grace is truly the solvent of sin's power. When sin comes in like a flood and threatens to destroy my soul, grace comes to the rescue and saves the day. Surely we should marvel more at His infinite, matchless grace; unearned, so undeserved, and so absolutely necessary in the character and purpose of God. One day we will see Him and we will probably follow John's example falling at His feet as dead. Jesus, true to character will lay His right hand on our shoulder and say: "… Fear not; I am the first and the last; I am he that liveth, and was dead; and, behold, I am alive forevermore, Amen …" (Rev. 1:17–18).

One of these days we shall see Him as he is, and as always, He will be full of grace and truth. I leave you with the last verse of the Bible: "The grace of our Lord Jesus Christ be with you all. Amen" (Rev. 22:21).

Chapter 7

CPSIA information can be obtained
at www.ICGtesting.com
Printed in the USA
FFOW05n1144210216